What people are saying...

HEROES LIVE HERE
A TRIBUTE TO CAMP PENDLETON MARINES SINCE 9/11

"This is our OIF and OEF coffee table book and is a compelling look back after more than 20 years of continuous combat operations. Amy captures history and personal stories of service and sacrifice. She expertly ties the book together with graphics and a map showcasing memorials throughout Camp Pendleton."

– Col. Riccoh Player, USMC Commanding Officer
OIF & OEF veteran and Emmy Award-winning producer

"Amy Forsythe brings to life the compelling backstories of the men and women who so bravely served in the U.S. military, laying down their lives for a country they loved. This powerful book brings out the humanness in the heroes that connect us all."

– Sandra Maas, veteran broadcast journalist and TV news anchor,
VP External Affairs at the Women's Museum of California

"Amy knows Camp Pendleton probably better than anyone. Her book is a shining example of how Marines honor the fallen."

– 1st Sgt. Dennis Walsh, USMC (Ret.), OEF and OIF veteran

"We must never forget the Marines and Sailors who have answered our nation's call for the past 20 years. This book is a remarkable testament to our heroes; America's sons and daughters, expertly told by a master storyteller with numerous combat deployments under her belt."

– Marty Schaeffer, Special Operations Public Affairs Officer

HEROES LIVE HERE

Ryan,
Thank you for your
service to our country
and U.S. Navy!

Semper Fidelis,

Aunjhe

HEROES LIVE HERE

A TRIBUTE TO CAMP PENDLETON MARINES SINCE 9/11

AMY FORSYTHE

FOREWORD BY LT. GEN. LAWRENCE D. NICHOLSON, USMC (RET.)

TwoPalms
MEDIA GROUP

Heroes Live Here: A Tribute to Camp Pendleton Marines Since 9/11

First published in the United States in 2021 by Two Palms Media Group.
Fallbrook, California, U.S.A.

Library of Congress Control Number: 2021917338

FORSYTHE, AMY, Author

HEROES LIVE HERE

AMY FORSYTHE

ISBN: 978-1-7375957-1-7 (hardcover)
ISBN: 978-1-7375957-0-0 (paperback)
ISBN: 978-1-7375957-3-1 (eBook)

Editor: Patricia "Trish" Beaulieu

Design and Production: Nancy Ratkiewich, NJR Productions

Graphic Artist: Dan Zimmerman, Devil Dog Graphix

Publishing Consultant: Susie Schaefer, Finish the Book Publishing

Photography: Amy Forsythe and additional sources

Historical photos: Courtesy of Camp Pendleton History and Museum Archives

PHOTOGRAPHY / Individual Photographers / Monographs
TRAVEL / Special Interest / Military

QUANTITY PURCHASES: Schools, companies, professional groups, clubs, and other organizations may qualify for special terms when ordering quantities of this title. For information, email heroesliveherecp@gmail.com.

Printed in the United States of America

10 9 8 7 6 5 4 3 2 1

COVER IMAGE: *U.S. Marines honor the fallen during a memorial service for Sgt. Joe L. Wrightsman at Patrol Base Jaker in Helmand Province, Afghanistan, July 30, 2010. (Photo by Sgt. Mark Fayloga)*

*This book is dedicated to the men and women
stationed at Camp Pendleton who've made
the ultimate sacrifice in service to
our nation since September 11, 2001.*

Semper Fidelis

TABLE OF CONTENTS

"Some people spend an entire
lifetime wondering if they made
a difference in the world. But,
the Marines don't have that problem."

—President Ronald Reagan, May 26, 1983

Lt. Gen. Lawrence D. Nicholson

FOREWORD

By Lieutenant General Lawrence D. Nicholson
U.S. Marine Corps (ret.)
Former 5th Marines and 1st Marine Division Commander

Since its founding in September of 1942, Marines and Sailors have deployed from Camp Pendleton, California, to conflicts around the globe. From the iconic battles of the Pacific Theater during WWII, to the Korean Peninsula, Vietnam, Desert Storm, and most recently from 2001 to today in Afghanistan and Iraq. Many thousands of Marines and Sailors from this great base have worn the cloth of our nation and served at the point of friction in every conflict.

Amy Forsythe is not only the author of this great book, *Heroes Live Here* she is also a Marine combat veteran whom I served with in Fallujah, Iraq, at the height of that war. Her insights and narratives are personal, sometimes painful but always real. Amy has that firsthand experience one can only acquire from time spent in a combat zone. The good days and the bad, the lost comrades and painful memorial services, the heart wrenching and heartwarming. Her brilliant research and ability to provide that first person account of not only the conflict, but the enduring support our Marines and their families received from the local communities that steadfastly supported them through two decades of deployments, is perhaps unique in our nation.

In 1980, as a young 2nd Lieutenant, fresh from the schools of Quantico, Virginia, I checked into Camp Pendleton. As a young infantry officer in 3rd Battalion, 1st Marine Regiment, 1st Marine Division, I learned to simulta-

neously love and hate the hills, trails, and beaches of this majestic base. The 17-mile stretch of pristine coastline that definitively separates San Diego County from the ever-expanding reach of Los Angeles sprawl is one of America's environmental treasures. Little did I know then that over the next 40 years, my love affair with this base would allow me to return many times over to include commanding both the 5th Marine Regiment in Iraq in 2006-2007, and ultimately the famed and legendary Blue Diamond itself (1st Marine Division) from 2013 to 2015.

This book is focused on the war years of 2001 to 2021 and the role, impact, and great sacrifices made by the Marines and Sailors of Camp Pendleton. While every military base and community around our nation was profoundly impacted by the attacks of September 11, 2001, Amy Forsythe brilliantly works to capture the impact at this one special place so many of us have at one time called home.

Heroes Live Here honors the great men and women of this generation who simply said "If not me, then who?" Young Americans who may never have served and were moved to service by the events of September 11th.

This book focuses on those young Americans who served at Camp Pendleton and the communities that supported them. Communities like Dana Point, San Clemente, Newport Beach, Carlsbad and so many others.

Communities who reached out and relentlessly took care of families of the deployed, hosted holiday functions for the children, mailed hundreds if not thousands of packages to the deployed warriors, and welcomed them home from deployments in a manner that would be envied by Roman Legionnaires. Communities that tirelessly worked with commanders like me to build Memorials to the fallen with private funding so that we would never forget the enormous sacrifice made by these heroes.

Amy Forsythe's book **Heroes Live Here** is an important addition to the distinguished list of written work that has been published on the Iraq and Afghan wars. Amy has shined a light on what I believe to be an underserved segment of these wars; and that is the bases, stations, and communities that trained, supported, deployed, and welcomed them back home. Thank you Amy for this important glimpse into a very personal and under-reported narrative of these past 20 years. Job well done, Marine, and job well done by those incredible communities who through the ups and downs of a 20 year conflict, never fatigued, never stood down, and never stopped selflessly serving the heroes and their families.

Semper Fidelis,

Lawrence D. Nicholson

Lawrence D. Nicholson
Lieutenant General, USMC (Ret.)

INTRODUCTION

BY AMY FORSYTHE
U.S. MARINE VETERAN AND FORMER COMBAT CORRESPONDENT

I was first stationed at Camp Pendleton in 1995 as a Marine combat correspondent and fell in love with the history, the landscape and the people that make this base one of the best places to live, work and play. Since 9/11, Marines and Sailors assigned to Camp Pendleton have played a large role in supporting combat operations in Afghanistan and Iraq.

Heroes Live Here: A Tribute to Camp Pendleton Marines Since 9/11 started as a passion project to share a few photos of the new memorials on base with friends and family. It's now turned into a mission to showcase the numerous new memorials and markers honoring our Marines and Sailors who were stationed at Camp Pendleton and deployed to Afghanistan and Iraq since 9/11 to a wider audience including Gold Star families, fellow Marines and others who are not able to visit the base.

Many of the stories captured in this book are from personal connections I've made over the past 25 years, having served five combat tours—two to Iraq and three to Afghanistan. These poignant accounts of honor, courage and commitment are a testament to the Corps' role in defending our national security.

Amy stands at the El Camino Real Commemorative Bell on Camp Pendleton. It's one of California's 500 historic El Camino Real bells placed throughout the state. The El Camino Real runs right through the heart of Camp Pendleton and the bell symbolizes the markers of the trail used by the Franciscan Padres on their journey to Northern California from Mexico in the 1800s.

My hope is that this book captures reflections and remembrances from those who were stationed at Camp Pendleton through the past two decades and who still have strong ties to the base. It was important for me to share the immense care and compassion our community partners have for raising funds and working to build places of honor on the installation, such as the **5th Marines Memorial Park and Garden** located at Camp Horno and the ***No Man Left Behind*** monument at the Wounded Warrior Complex.

The book also includes reflections from: a Navy Cross recipient, the author of ***Sergeant Rex: The Unbreakable Bond Between a Marine and His Military Working Dog*** and a Marine combat artist who was on assignment during the height of the combat operations in Iraq in 2006.

Camp Pendleton has been home to several generations of Marines, Sailors, and their families since it's opening in 1942. The base is rich with history and has a legacy that continues to thrive with each passing year.

It's the West Coast's premiere expeditionary training installation and provides exceptional training facilities for many active-duty and reserve Marine, Navy, and Army units, as well as national, state and local agencies. The base is committed to being good stewards of its natural resources, preserving archaeological sites, restoring historical military buildings and protecting endangered species.

Located about an hour north of San Diego, the surrounding communities of Oceanside, Carlsbad, Vista, San Marcos, San Clemente, Dana Point, Temecula, and Murrieta, play an integral role for partnerships in the region and continue to support our Marines and veteran communities.

There's a saying that "home is where the Marine Corps sends you" and for those lucky enough, we can be grateful for a place like Camp Pendleton that honors heroes of every generation. For all those who serve and support Marines, Sailors, and their family members at Camp Pendleton, I salute you.

Semper Fidelis,

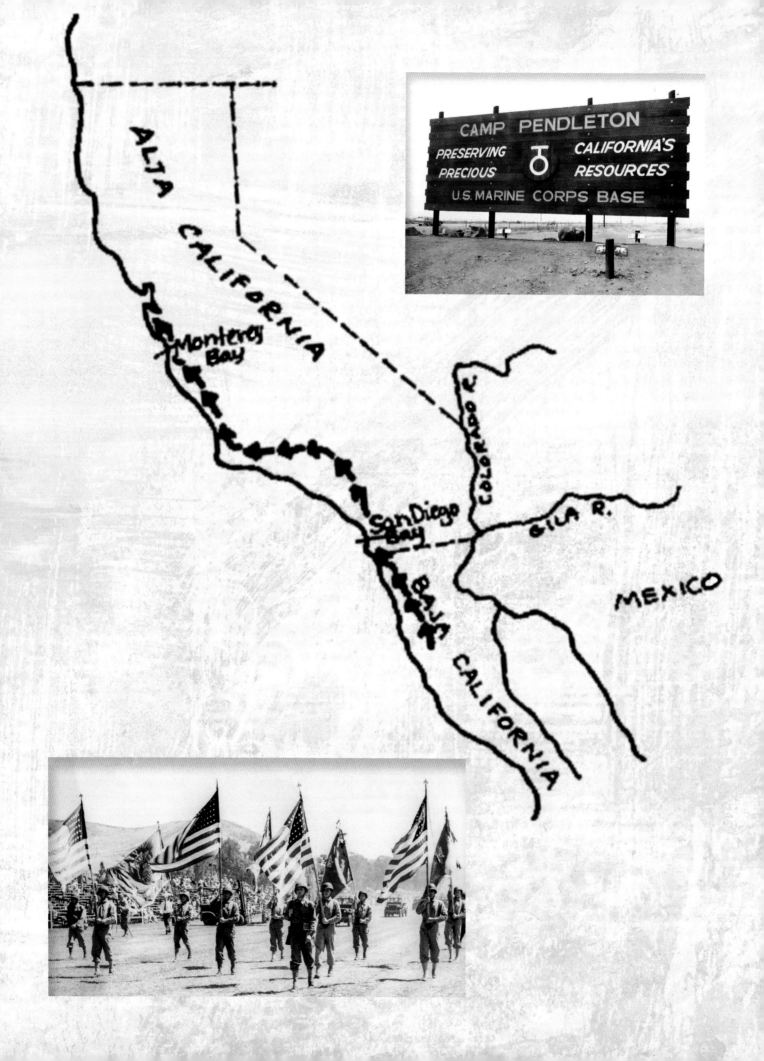

ALTA CALIFORNIA

Monterey Bay

San Diego Bay

BAJA CALIFORNIA

COLORADO R.

GILA R.

MEXICO

CAMP PENDLETON
PRESERVING CALIFORNIA'S
PRECIOUS RESOURCES
U.S. MARINE CORPS BASE

CHAPTER 1

HISTORY OF CAMP PENDLETON

Of all the Marine Corps bases throughout the world, Camp Pendleton has one of the most intriguing pasts, filled with historical charm and vibrancy. Spanish explorers, colorful politicians, herds of thundering cattle, skillful vaqueros, and tough Marines have all contributed to the history of this land.

In 1769, a Spaniard by the name of Captain Gaspar de Portola led an expeditionary force northward from lower California, seeking to establish Franciscan missions throughout California. On July 20 of that same year, the expedition arrived at a location now known as Camp Pendleton, and as it was the holy day St. Margaret, they baptized the land in the name of Santa Margarita.

During the next 30 years, 21 missions were established, the most productive one being Mission San Luis Rey, just south of the present-day Camp Pendleton. At that time, San Luis Rey Mission had control over the Santa Margarita area.

In 1821, following Mexico's independence from Spain, the Californios became the new ruling class of California, and many were the first generation descendants of the Portola expedition. The Mexican governor was awarding land grants and ranchos to prominent businessmen, officials, and military leaders.

Pio Pico was a prominent politician, ranchero, and entrepreneur, famous for serving as the last Governor of Alta California (present-day California) under Mexican rule.

LIFE ON THE RANCHO

In 1841, two brothers by the name of Pio and Andres Pico became the first private owners of Rancho Santa Margarita. More land was later added to the grant, making the name Rancho Santa Margarita y Las Flores, and that name stayed with the ranch until the Marine Corps acquired it in 1942.

In 1863, a dashing Englishman named John Forster (Pio Pico's brother-in-law) paid off Pico's gambling debts in return for the deed to the ranch. During his tenure as owner of the ranch, he expanded the ranch house, which was begun by the Picos in 1841, and developed the rancho into a thriving cattle industry.

Forster's heirs, however, were forced to sell the ranch in 1882 because of a string of bad luck, which included a series of droughts and a fence law that forced Forster to construct fencing around the extensive rancho lands. It was purchased by wealthy cattleman James Flood and managed by Irishman Richard O'Neill who was eventually rewarded for his faithful service with half ownership.

Under the guidance of O'Neill's son, Jerome, the ranch began to net a profit of nearly half a million dollars annually, and the house was modernized and furnished to its present form.

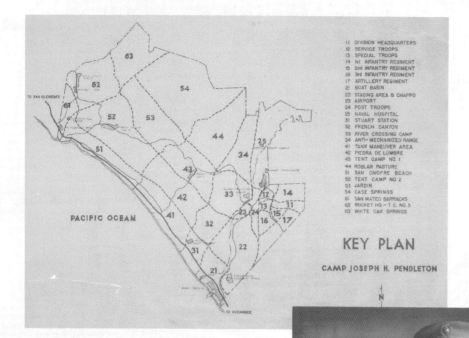

11 DIVISION HEADQUARTERS
12 SERVICE TROOPS
13 SPECIAL TROOPS
14 1st INFANTRY REGIMENT
15 2nd INFANTRY REGIMENT
16 3rd INFANTRY REGIMENT
17 ARTILLERY REGIMENT
21 BOAT BASIN
22 STAGING AREA & CHAPPO
23 AIRPORT
24 POST TROOPS
25 NAVAL HOSPITAL
31 STUART STATION
32 FRENCH CANYON
33 RIVER CROSSING CAMP
34 ANTI-MECHANIZED RANGE
41 TANK MANEUVER AREA
42 PIEDRA DE LUMBRE
43 TENT CAMP NO. 1
44 ROBLAR PASTURE
51 SAN ONOFRE BEACH
52 TENT CAMP NO 2
53 JARDIN
54 CASE SPRINGS
61 SAN MATEO BARRACKS
62 ROCKET HQ.— T.C. NO.3
63 WHITE OAK SPRINGS

KEY PLAN

CAMP JOSEPH H. PENDLETON

PACIFIC OCEAN

Born in Rochester, Pennsylvania, on June 2, 1860, "Uncle Joe" Pendleton, as he would later be known, graduated from the U. S. Naval Academy and was commissioned a second lieutenant in the U. S. Marine Corps on July 1, 1884.

Pendleton/Brown Collection

In the early 1940s, both the Army and the Marine Corps were looking for land for a large training base. The Army lost interest in the project, but in April of 1942 it was announced that the rancho was about to be transformed into the largest Marine Corps base in the country. The Marine Corps paid $4,239,062 for the rancho.

Following the purchase of the vast Rancho Santa Margarita y Las Flores in 1942, the new West Coast Marine Corps training base would be named for Maj. Gen. Joseph Henry Pendleton, who had pioneered Marine Corps activities in the San Diego area during his 46 years of distinguished service from 1878 to 1924. Pendleton's service included duty in the jungles of Nicaragua, Santa Domingo, Guam, and the Philippines, in addition to several stateside and shipboard tours.

After he retired, Pendleton bought a house in Coronado near the harbor and became active in the civic affairs of the city. He served as mayor of Coronado from 1928 to 1930. Married to the former Mary Helen Fay, he died in San Diego in 1942 at the age of 81.

The Corps broadened its capabilities during the 1980s from "amphibious" to "expeditionary" by combining infantry, armor, supply and air force. Troops and equipment could now be deployed halfway around the world in only days as part of a self-sustaining air-ground team. This successful use of military power has been demonstrated through Marine Corps operations in Grenada, Panama, the Persian Gulf, Somalia, Bosnia, Haiti, Afghanistan, and Iraq. Camp Pendleton has continued to grow through renovations, replacing its original tent camps with more than 2,600 buildings and 500 miles of roads.

In 1975, Vietnamese resettlement camps were established at Camp Pendleton as part of Operation New Arrivals, the largest humanitarian airlift in history. The northern part of the base was used for housing, feeding, and processing more than 50,000 Vietnamese refugees from May through November in 1975.

Hundreds of Quonset huts were built as more Marines were assigned to the new west coast base.

Greetings from CAMP Joseph H. PENDLETON California

Since its founding in September of 1942, Marines and Sailors have deployed from Camp Pendleton, California, to conflicts around the globe. From the iconic battles of the Pacific theater during WWII, to the Korean Peninsula, Vietnam, Desert Storm, and most recently from 2001 to today in Afghanistan and Iraq.

The first troops to occupy the new base were the 9th Marine Regiment with the 1st Battalion, 12th Marines, who marched from Camp Elliott in San Diego to Camp Pendleton in 1942.

Opposite page: President Franklin D. Roosevelt dedicated the base on Sept. 25, 1942, in honor of World War I Major General Joseph H. Pendleton, who had long advocated establishing a west coast training base.

The first contingent of 95 female Marines arrived at Camp Pendleton on Oct. 26, 1943, a little over a year after the base was dedicated in 1942.

Photo courtesy of Camp Pendleton History and Museum Archives

Preserving History — The Ranch House Today

SANTA MARGARITA RANCH HOUSE COMPLEX

The site was listed on the National Register of Historic Places in 1971, including the main ranch house, the Bunkhouse, Chapel, and 21 acres of associated grounds. The buildings are examples of Spanish Colonial/Mexican California architecture mainly constructed in the 19th century. The main ranch house served as headquarters of one of the largest ranchos in California until 1942, when the U.S. government acquired approximately 125,000 acres of rancho lands and converted the site to a military base.

Historically known as the **Rancho Santa Margarita y Las Flores,** the site acquired its present form while the ranch was under the management of some of the most notable figures in California history, including Pio Pico, the last Mexican governor of Alta California, Juan Forster, a prominent rancher and Pico's brother-in-law, and Richard O'Neill, whose family operated the ranch for nearly 60 years beginning in 1882. Until recently, the base commanding general and his family lived in the home but has since been vacated to better preserve the structures.

The original ranch house is used for historical tours and has been declared a National Historic Site. Some of the base's streets and sites have been named in honor of military war heroes and battles. The "T & O" was used as the rancho's cattle brand for many years and can still be seen throughout the base on many signs and markings as a tribute to the base's rich history.

Tours of the Santa Margarita Ranch House complex (Ranch House, Chapel, and Bunkhouse Museum) are available by appointment only on the first Tuesday, first Thursday, and second Thursday of the month by the Rancho Santa Margarita y Las Flores Docents. To sign up for a tour, please contact the History Museum Branch by phone at (760) 725-5758 and email: mcbcampen_history@usmc.mil. Learn more at: camppendletonranchhouse.org.

Photo courtesy of Camp Pendleton History and Museum Archives

The Ranch House Chapel is the oldest structure on the base, having started out as a winery in 1810 when the land belonged to Mission San Luis Rey. It was severely damaged by heavy rains and flooding in 1993. The Chapel was carefully restored in 1994 thanks to private donations which played a significant role in the restoration project.

CHAPTER 2

HOME IS WHERE THE MARINE CORPS SENDS YOU

Camp Pendleton is home to approximately 45,000 active duty Marines and Sailors. Generations of Marines have served here and now have a collective place to visit and share memories. The Camp Pendleton Veterans Memorial Garden was dedicated on Aug. 21, 2003.

The garden honors historical actions or events of significance on behalf of active military units and veterans' organizations. The gardens contain many plants native to the region and are maintained by Marines, the Navy and civilian volunteers. The garden is located across from the Pacific Views Events Center and overlooks the ocean, serving as a quiet place for reflection.

VETERANS MEMORIAL GARDENS AT PACIFIC VIEWS

FROM THE GARDEN

The gardens contain a unique selection of plants that are native to the region, such as Ceanothus (creeping mountain lilac), Big Sur Manzanita, California Sunflower, Red Buckwheat, Deer Grass, Dwarf Coyote Bush, Lemonade Berry, Toyon, California Sycamore and the Coast Live Oak. The garden and memorials are maintained by Marines, Navy, and civilian volunteers.

KOREAN WAR MONUMENT

The Chosin Few monument, located in the Camp Pendleton Veterans Memorial Garden, was dedicated honoring the service and sacrifices of Korean War veterans at Camp Pendleton Sept. 15, 2010.

The 6-by-8 foot, 3,000-pound granite monument sits among other memorials at the garden with a sweeping view of the Pacific Ocean at the Pacific Views Event Center near the base's main gate. It is dedicated to "We Few, We Chosin Few, We Eternal Band of Brothers." The garden honors historical actions and events of significance on behalf of active military units and veteran organizations.

The War Dawgs memorial, which is located in the Camp Pendleton Veterans Memorial Garden, was unveiled Aug. 9, 2014, in the garden south of the Pacific Views Event Center not far from the Naval Hospital Camp Pendleton.

The dedication ceremony included a reading of the names of 312 dog handlers killed in action in Vietnam and those killed in Iraq and Afghanistan. The 5,000-pound monument is the first of its kind in the memorial garden to pay tribute to K-9 military members.

A group of veterans and patriots who developed the memorial from the Dawgs Project wanted to pay tribute to fallen "Dawgs," as the handlers call themselves, and their heroic canine companions with whom they go into combat.

Dogs have gone to the battlefield, carrying supplies and messages, tracking enemies, sniffing for bombs and guarding their human comrades, according to the Dawgs Project co-founder Jon Hemp, a dog handler with the Air Force during the Vietnam War. The 6-foot black granite monument commemorates the services of K-9 units of all military branches dating back to WWI.

Deep thanks and gratitude from Angels Without Wings, Inc. &
Camp Pendleton Historical Society
Sponsors & Donors
Timothy T Day Foundation, Inc.
Anne & Tony Joseph   Perot Foundation
Mary & Gary West   Judith Burns
Barbara Wong   Karen & Michael Storms
Chairman Yong Chu Park   Michael & Reva Mason*
Warner & Debra Lusardi   John & Carol Newsom*
Forrest & Sally Haglund   Kenneth Latham*
Del Mar Thoroughbred Club Sgt Reckless Fan Club
Dana Point 8th Marine Regiment Support Group
Team Reckless
Robin L Hutton: Founder   Harold Wadley: Advisor*
Jocelyn L Russelli: Artist Robert L Rogers: Coordinator*
Richard B Rothwell   Rick Burroughs   Warren & Lori Wilson   Col Jina McCain*
*Served with SSgt Reckless

Deep thanks and gratitude from Angels Without Wings, Inc. &
Camp Pendleton Historical Society
Sponsors & Donors

Timothy T Day Foundation, Inc.

Anne & Tony Joseph · Perot Foundation
Mary & Gary West · Judith Burns

Barbara Wong · Karen & Michael Storms
Chairman Yong Chu Park · Michael & Reva Mason*
Warner & Debra Lusardi · John & Carol Newsom*
Forrest & Sally Hoglund · Kenneth Latham*
Del Mar Thoroughbred Club · Sgt Reckless Fan Club
Dana Point 5th Marine Regiment Support Group

Team Reckless

Robin L Hutton: Founder · Harold Wadley: Advisor*
Jocelyn L Russell: Artist · Robert L Rogers: Coordinator*

Richard B Rothwell · Rick Burroughs · Warren & Lori Wilson · Col Jinx McCain*

*Served with SSgt Reckless

STAFF SERGEANT RECKLESS

When you first arrive at the Veterans Memorial Garden on Marine Corps Base Camp Pendleton, you are greeted by the Staff Sergeant Reckless monument. The life-like statue was unveiled on Oct. 26, 2016, in honor of the Korean War packhorse whose numerous awards include two Purple Hearts, a Marine Corps Good Conduct Medal, and the National Defense Service Medal.

Linda Sundram is the founder and President of Pendleton Community Service Fund, a 501(c)(3) charity that supports humanitarian causes in the United States and internationally. Her small club provided the Palomar College Foundation with a $50,000 gift for educational scholarships. Her Generation to Generation program picks up furniture on base five days a week and 50 weeks a year. In the last 10 years, she has transferred about $35 million in household furnishing to more than 100,000 military families free of charge.

Prior to retirement, she was Manager of the New York City Insurance Claims office of the Travelers Insurance Company. She has been honored as the "Volunteer of the Year" by the San Diego Military Advisory Council—an alliance of Employers, Military, and City Leadership.

With our deepest gratitude for their sacrifice, this Memorial was given to the Marines and Sailors of Camp Pendleton by:

The Rotary Club of Bonsall
The Rotary Club of Camp Pendleton
The Rotary Club of Carlsbad
The Rotary Club of Escondido East
The Rotary Club of Escondido Sunrise
The Rotary Club of Valley Center
The Rotary Club of Vista

I MARINE EXPEDITIONARY FORCE MEMORIAL WALL

The I Marine Expeditionary Force Memorial Wall was unveiled and dedicated by Lt. Gen. Thomas Waldhauser on Feb. 1, 2012. More than 1,200 names of Marines who died in Iraq and Afghanistan since 9/11 are engraved on the curving stone wall located across the street from the 1st Marine Division headquarters building in Mainside at Camp Pendleton.

"All of the soldiers, airmen, Navy and Marines have been volunteers. They left their families behind, knowing full well that serving their country could come at the expense of their lives," Waldhauser said at the dedication ceremony. Waldhauser noted that the first names on the wall are a six-person unit from Camp Pendleton who died in Pakistan in 2002 who were some of the very first combat casualties of Operation Enduring Freedom.

The memorial was spearheaded by Linda Sundram, Chair of Camp Pendleton Rotary, a satellite of the Rotary Club of Carlsbad (the first Rotary Club chartered on a military base). It was presented as a gift from Rotary members from Bonsall, Camp Pendleton, Vista, Valley Center, Carlsbad, and Escondido. The Marine Corps paid an estimated $65,000. Lighting, concrete and other materials were donated for the project.

2005 2006

OPERATION IRAQI FREEDOM

2003 - 2011

Adam A. Galvez, OIF
Paul J. Darga, OIF

Joseph T. McCloud, OIF
Thomas P. Echols, OIF
Megan M. McClung, OIF
Cody G. Watson, OIF
Dustin J. Libby, OIF

Jared M. Shoemaker, OIF
Eric P. Valdepenas, OIF
Vincent M. Frassetto, OIF
Johnathan L. Benson, OIF
Ryan A. Miller, OIF
Christopher M. Zimmerman, OIF
Yull Estrada Rodriguez, OIF
Howard S. March, OIF
Rene Martinez, OIF
Christopher T. Riviere, OIF

Clifford R. Collinsw
Nathan R. Elrow
Joshua C. Watki
Eric W. Herzberr
Charles O. Sar
Richard A. Buerst
Tyler R. Overstre
Charles V. Komp
onathan B. Thorns
Thomas M. Gilb
Daniel B. Chaire
Donald S. Brow
Luke J. Zimmem
Troy D. Nealey
Gary A. Koehle
Minhee Kim,
James E. Brow
Michael H. Lasl
Luke B. Holler
Jason D. Whiteho
Mark C. Gelina
Kyle W. Powe
Jose A. Galva
Ryan T. McCaug
Bryan K. Burge

2007   2008   200

OPERATION ENDURING FREEDOM
2001 -

2002

Daniel G. McCollum, OEF
Matthew W. Bancroft, OEF
Stephen L. Bryson, OEF
Bryan P. Bertrand, OEF
Jeannette L. Winters, OEF
Nathan P. Hays, OEF
Scott N. Germosen, OEF
Walter F. Cohee, OEF
Dwight J. Morgan, OEF

Names of those service members killed in Afghanistan and Iraq who served under the I Marine Expeditionary Force are etched in the stone panels. The names are listed under the year they were killed beginning with the first seven Marines who died on Jan. 9, 2002, when the KC-130 military refueling plane they were riding in crashed into a mountainside as it prepared to land at a forward operating base in western Pakistan. Among those killed was radio operator Sgt. Jeannette L. Winters, 25, of Gary, Indiana, the first woman to be killed in the U.S.-led war on terrorism under Operation Enduring Freedom.

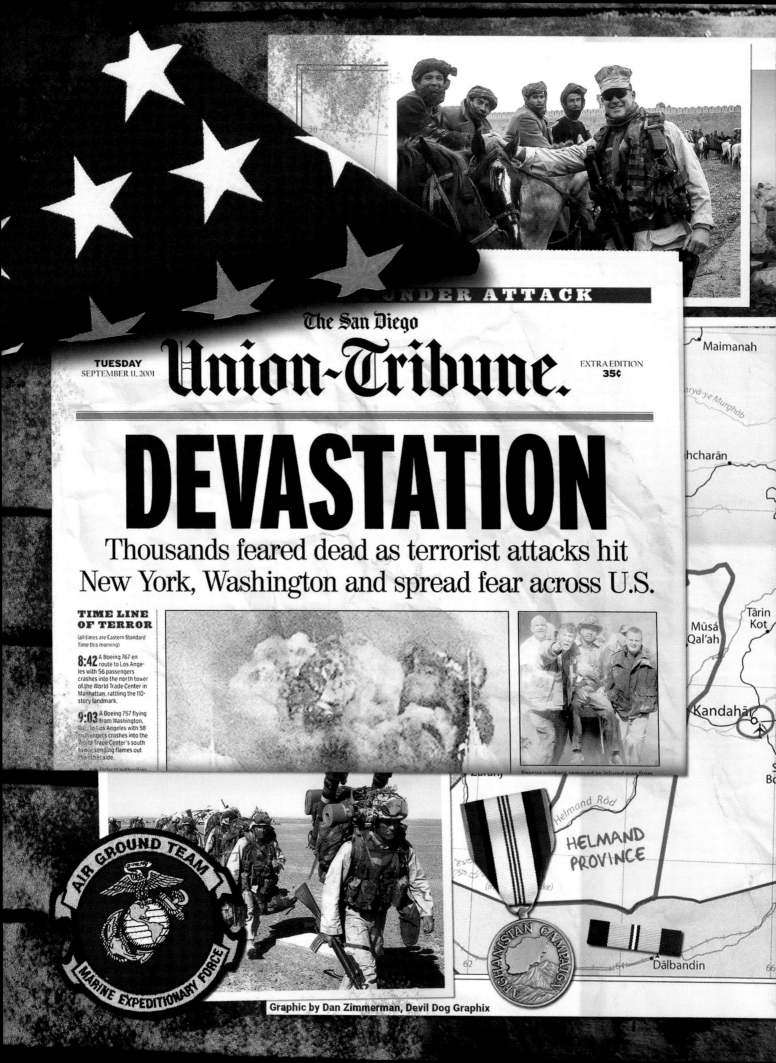

UNDER ATTACK

The San Diego
Union-Tribune.

TUESDAY
SEPTEMBER 11, 2001

EXTRA EDITION
35¢

DEVASTATION
Thousands feared dead as terrorist attacks hit New York, Washington and spread fear across U.S.

TIME LINE OF TERROR

(all times are Eastern Standard Time this morning)

8:42 A Boeing 767 en route to Los Angeles with 56 passengers crashes into the north tower of the World Trade Center in Manhattan, rattling the 110-story landmark.

9:03 A Boeing 757 flying from Washington, D.C. to Los Angeles with 58 passengers crashes into the World Trade Center's south tower, sending flames out the other side.

Maimanah

hcharān

Tārin Kot

Mūsá Qal'ah

Kandahār

Helmand Rōd

HELMAND PROVINCE

Dālbandin

Graphic by Dan Zimmerman, Devil Dog Graphix

OPERATION ENDURING FREEDOM

BLUE DIAMOND MEMORIAL AT 1ST MARINE DIVISION HEADQUARTERS

Located in front of the 1st Marine Division headquarters building, this memorial was dedicated to the Marines and Sailors of 1st Marine Division who made the ultimate sacrifice in support of Operation Enduring Freedom in Afghanistan.

The memorial was built in Afghanistan and brought back to California when Marines left. It's situated on the southwest side of the front of the Division's headquarters building in the 11 Area of Camp Pendleton. The storied unit's emblem, a blue diamond with five white stars and red number one with the word Guadalcanal listed vertically, is centered on top of the U.S. and Afghanistan flags, along with dog tags hanging on each side. There's also a memorial plaque embedded into the glass and dedicated to Division Marines who served in Afghanistan from 2001 to 2021.

The 1st Marine Division headquarters building is known colloquially as "The White House" and has been the command post of the 1st Marine Division since 1946. Built in 1943, it was constructed as a temporary structure, originally intended to stand for five years. Instead it has seen the Division through almost every American military engagement since then.

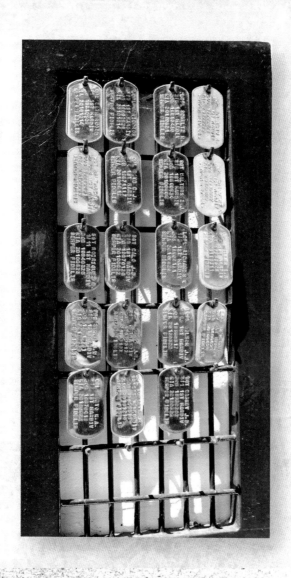

THIS MEMORIAL IS DEDICATED
TO THE MARINES AND SAILORS OF THE
1ST MARINE DIVISION
WHO FOUGHT IN AFGHANISTAN
DURING OPERATION
"ENDURING FREEDOM", AND THOSE
WHO FOUGHT AND GAVE THEIR LIVES
DURING OPERATION "IRAQI FREEDOM".
DEDICATED ON 29 JANUARY 2004
BY THE 1ST MARINE DIVISION ASSOCIATION

THE SEMPER FI SPIRIT LIVES ON

by Sgt. Maj. Justin Lehew, USMC (Ret.)

You will see all the best that America has to offer at Camp Pendleton. American men and women have admirably answered the nation's call from within her borders since 1942. When the nation needed them the most, they have always said "Send me, I will go." The post 9/11 generation of warfighters were born out of the terrorist attacks on our country on Sept. 11, 2001.

They were an all-volunteer force. They were your sons, daughters, husbands, wives, brothers, sisters, uncles, nieces, cousins, friends, and neighbors. Ordinary Americans who, when called upon, performed extraordinary things in the most challenging of circumstances, in the most hostile of environments.

In a day and age when there are those who feel that Americans are not what they once were, you will see on Camp Pendleton all that is still right and good about our nation on display. Each person trained and deployed from here has a different story, but there is one binding principle that resonates across all and is undeniably clear. The American fighting man and woman who called Camp Pendleton home during the post 9/11 era is clearly the yardstick from which all other fighting forces continue to be measured from. It's the reason a lot of us still bleed the red, white and blue of the Blue Diamond today and are extremely proud of our service in it.

The fighting spirit that was cultivated in generations before on this base is alive and well in the hills, waterways, and training expanses of her today. The legacy of those men and women who came before and trained here continue to inspire those today to do their part to ensure they do not let those who have come before them down. The same brother and sisterhood, spirit, service, heroism, and sacrifice that you will find spanning the illustrious battle history of our Corps from Tripoli, Bladensburg, Chapultepec, Mobile Bay, Vera Cruz, Belleau Wood, Peleliu, Chosin, Hue City, Kuwait and Somalia is still found here in spades and always will be.

American Marines and Sailors of my generation have proven themselves very worthy successors to those who have come before and worn the cloth of our nation. Woven forever more into this fabric of our battle history, names like Kandahar, Nasiriyah, Najaf, Fallujah, Ramadi, Al Qaim, Marjah and Sangin will echo through the ages and inspire the current and next generation of fighting men and women of our nation, who will be training and preparing for war from Camp Pendleton.

There is not a day that goes by that I do not fondly recall memories from my time spent at Camp Pendleton. I consider myself one of the luckiest men to have ever worn the uniform in the history of the Marines, in part because of my service here and how that time in my life greatly shaped the man I am today. It has a lot to do with the reason my phone ringer to this very day still plays "Waltzing Matilda."

Semper Fidelis,

Justin LeHew

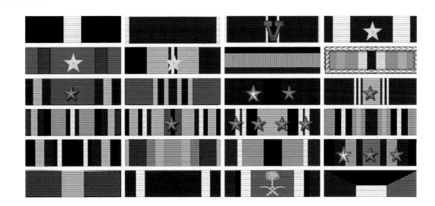

About Justin: Justin LeHew serves as the Chief Operating Officer for the world's most successful private MIA search and recovery organization, History Flight, a charitable non-profit dedicated to the search, recovery and repatriation of America's missing in action from around the globe.

Justin is the son of an Army veteran who stormed Omaha Beach with the 29th Infantry Division in France on D-Day, June 6, 1944. Justin served 31 years in the U.S. Marine Corps following high school, retiring at the rank of Sergeant Major and serving as the enlisted head of the U.S. Marine Corps' Training and Education Command.

During his distinguished career, he served in the Assault Amphibian, Infantry and Reconnaissance fields, as well as a Marine Drill Instructor and Chief Academics Instructor. He served in combat actions around the globe ranging from Operation Desert Storm in 1991, Bosnia-Herzegovina in 1993 and multiple tours during the War on Terror in Iraq between 2003-2010.

Justin is also a dynamic and highly requested public speaker around the globe on management, motivation, and leadership and is one of the most highly decorated United States Marines who has served since the War on Terror began in 2003. He has been awarded the nation's second highest award for combat valor, the Navy Cross, for heroic actions in Iraq in 2003 and was awarded the Bronze Star for Valor in combat actions in Iraq again in 2004.

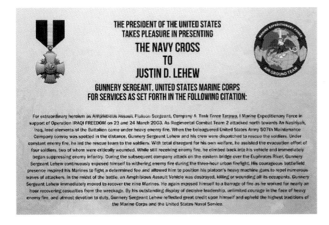

U.S. Marine 2nd Lt. Christopher Netley, 1st Marine Division (Forward), supply officer, stands at attention, as the commander of troops for the Colors and Memorial Dedication ceremony held aboard Camp Leatherneck, Afghanistan, Sept. 16, 2010, as a bell is rung for each fallen hero. The memorial ceremony was held in honor of the fallen heroes of 1st Marine Division lost while in support of the Operation Enduring Freedom. (Photo by Sgt. Ezekiel Kitandwe, 1st Marine Division)

CHAPTER 3

IF THESE HILLS COULD TALK

As the efforts to remove Saddam Hussein from power in Iraq, the Pentagon looked to the 1st Marine Division to prepare for the "Road to War." Then, Maj. Gen. James N. Mattis was the division commander and was well-respected by members of other services and had been at the forefront of a number of engagements.

Mattis led his battalion of Marines in the assault during the first Gulf war in 1991, and commanded the task force charging into Afghanistan in 2001. In 2003, he once again took up the task of motivating his young Marines to go into battle.

One day before beginning the assault into Iraq, on March 19, 2003, every member of 1st Marine Division received a letter.

In the letter, he tells them, "you are the world's most feared and trusted force." He conveys a sense of staying together and working as a team, writing, "keep faith in your comrades on your left and right and Marine Air overhead. Fight with a happy heart and a strong spirit."

He signed off with the motto of 1st Marine Division: "Demonstrate to the world that there's 'No Better Friend, No Worse Enemy,' than a U.S. Marine. The 1st Marine Division is the ground combat element of the I Marine Expeditionary Force.

Camp Pendleton's ridgeline overlooking Lake O'Neill at sunset. The highest summit on base is Margarita Peak, with an elevation of 3,136 feet.

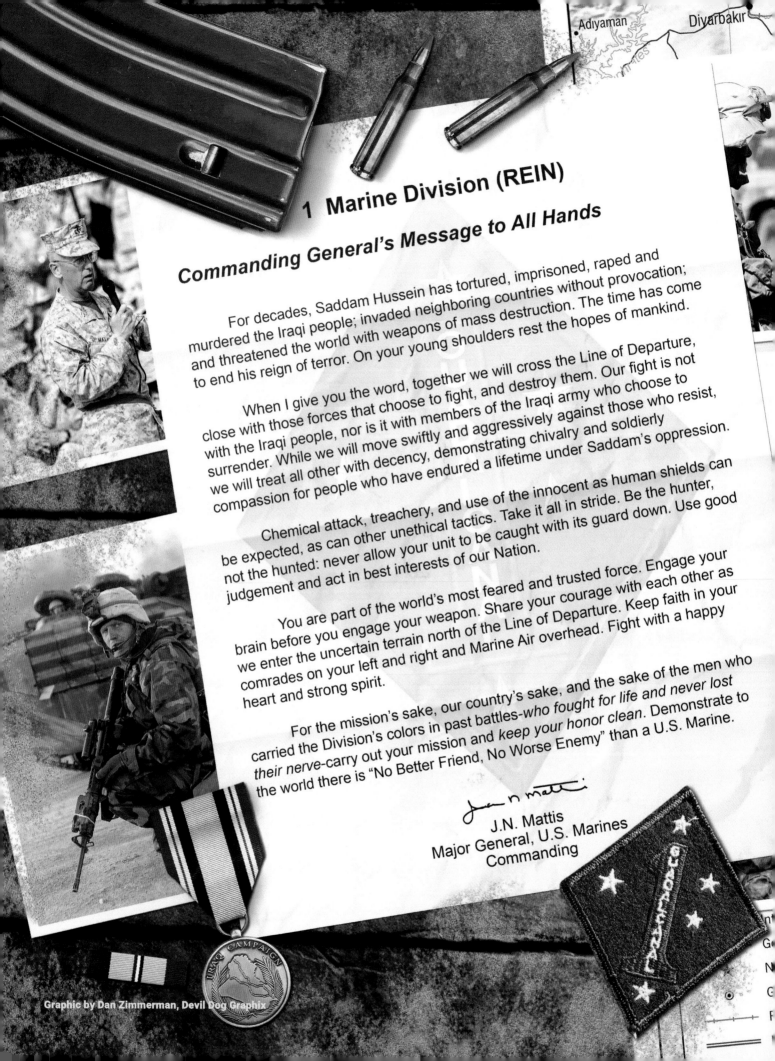

1 Marine Division (REIN)

Commanding General's Message to All Hands

For decades, Saddam Hussein has tortured, imprisoned, raped and murdered the Iraqi people; invaded neighboring countries without provocation; and threatened the world with weapons of mass destruction. The time has come to end his reign of terror. On your young shoulders rest the hopes of mankind.

When I give you the word, together we will cross the Line of Departure, close with those forces that choose to fight, and destroy them. Our fight is not with the Iraqi people, nor is it with members of the Iraqi army who choose to surrender. While we will move swiftly and aggressively against those who resist, we will treat all other with decency, demonstrating chivalry and soldierly compassion for people who have endured a lifetime under Saddam's oppression.

Chemical attack, treachery, and use of the innocent as human shields can be expected, as can other unethical tactics. Take it all in stride. Be the hunter, not the hunted: never allow your unit to be caught with its guard down. Use good judgement and act in best interests of our Nation.

You are part of the world's most feared and trusted force. Engage your brain before you engage your weapon. Share your courage with each other as we enter the uncertain terrain north of the Line of Departure. Keep faith in your comrades on your left and right and Marine Air overhead. Fight with a happy heart and strong spirit.

For the mission's sake, our country's sake, and the sake of the men who carried the Division's colors in past battles-who fought for life and never lost their nerve-carry out your mission and keep your honor clean. Demonstrate to the world there is "No Better Friend, No Worse Enemy" than a U.S. Marine.

J.N. Mattis
Major General, U.S. Marines
Commanding

"NO BETTER FRIEND, NO WORSE ENEMY."
- MAJ. GEN. JAMES MATTIS, USMC

1st Marines —
In the Heart of Camp Pendleton

Camp Pendleton's vast hills serve as one of the best training opportunities for our forces and have prepared generations of warfighters for a variety of missions. "If These Hills Could Talk" chapter is filled with memorials and stories of those who have trained here to be the fighting force our nation needs.

1ST MARINES MEMORIAL PARK

The 1st Marines Memorial Park and Garden was established in 2013 and was spearheaded by the Rotary Club of Camp Pendleton. The one-acre garden, with desert landscaping and mountain views, provides a quiet place to remember heroes of the regiment. The Memorial Park is a gathering place where many memories are made including celebrations and promotion.

2nd BATTALION 1st MARINES

OPERATION IRAQI FREEDOM

COMPANY E

LCPL	JOSEANTONIO GUTIERREZ	03/21/2003	LCPL	BRAD S. SHUDER	04/12/2004
LCPL	ROBERT P. ZURHEIDE JR.	04/12/2004	LCPL	AARON C. AUSTIN	04/26/2004
CPL	DEAN P. PRATT	08/02/2004	MAJ	RAY J. MENDOZA JR.	11/14/2005

COMPANY F

PFC	LEROY C. SANDOVAL JR.	03/26/2004	LCPL	BRANDON C. STURDY	05/13/2004
LCPL	JAMES B. HUSTON JR.	07/02/2004	PFC	DAVID P. BURRIDGE	09/06/2004
CPL	JOSPEH C. McCARTHY	09/06/2004	LCPL	MICHAEL J. ALLRED	09/06/2004
LCPL	LAMONT N. WILSON	09/06/2004	LCPL	QUINN A. KEITH	09/06/2004
CPL	CHRISTOPHER S. EBERT	09/17/2004	CPL	MICK R. NYGARDBEKOWSKY	11/06/2004
LCPL	CHRISTOPHER M. McCRACKIN	11/14/2005	CPL	JOHN M. LONGORIA	11/14/2005
LCPL	ROGER W. DEEDS	11/16/2005	1STLT	DONALD R. McGLOTHLIN	11/16/2005
LCPL	JOHN A. LUCENTE	11/16/2005	CPL	JEFFRY A. ROGERS	11/16/2005
BTN	ROBERT J. WARE	11/16/2005			

COMPANY G

CPL	MATTHEW E. MATULA	04/09/2004	LCPL	PHILLIP E. FRANK	04/08/2004

WEAPONS COMPANY

LCPL	SETH HUSTON	04/09/2004

HEADQUARTERS & SERVICE COMPANY

LCPL	CHRISTOPHER M POSTON	10/17/2005

COMBAT ENGINEERS

CPL	TYLER R. FEY	04/05/2004

OPERATION ENDURING FREEDOM

COMPANY E

CPL	CHAD S. WADE	12/01/2010

It provides a quiet place to remember the heroes of the 1st Marines. The centerpiece of the garden is a bronze statue of a field cross honoring the fallen that includes a rifle positioned between a pair of boots with a helmet on top of the weapon's buttstock. Plaques throughout the garden memorialize battalions within the regiment.

The garden, four years in the making, was spearheaded by Linda Sundram of the Rotary Club of Camp Pendleton, with additional funding from community members and businesses along with several other area Rotary clubs, including Valley Center, Escondido, and Oceanside clubs. The garden is on Basilone Road near the Single Marine Recreation Center at Camp Horno.

HORNO CROSSES ON THE HILL AT SUNRISE

The famous 'Horno Crosses' adorn a hilltop overlooking the center of Camp Pendleton, and serve as a sanctum for Marines honoring their fallen brothers and sisters. The first cross was set up by a small group of Marines with 2nd Battalion, 1st Marines, in 2003. While it's hard to reach, many make the trek up the steep hill and have left momentos over the years. *(Photo courtesy of Frank Sellin)*

A large group of veteran's from 1/9 "The Walking Dead" and other battalions from across Camp Pendleton carried this cross up to the top on April 29, 2018. The group included veterans from Vietnam, the first Gulf War, Somalia, Operation Iraqi Freedom, and Operation Enduring Freedom. (Photo courtesy of Frank Sellin)

U.S. Marines from 1st Battalion, 4th Marine Regiment, hike their way to a memorial site set up just outside of Camp Horno, April 26, 2005. The site was made in memory of Marines that died in support of Operation Iraqi Freedom. (Photo by U.S. Marine Cpl. Matthew S. Richards)

In 2003, U.S. Navy Chaplain Scott Radestki (above center) and six other service members climbed the hill as part of the original group that brought the crosses up the 3,000-foot trek. Through the years, there's been a swirling controversy about the unsanctioned memorials. Radestski commented several years ago that he was frustrated about the debate because some military officials wanted the crosses removed because they weren't approved through proper channels. "Those individuals who have poured out their life, poured out their hope, left those rock stones as mementos at the top of the hill to honor their fallen comrades and to get rid of the burdens and the sadness and frustration," Radestki told the media in 2012. (Courtesy photos)

(Right) Marines carry a cross up a hill to replace memorials after they were burned in a fire on base.

5TH MARINES MEMORIAL PARK AND GARDEN

The 5th Marines Memorial Park was established by Dana Point 5th Marine Regiment Support Group in 2008 and is a revered site where families, fellow Marines, and those who wish to pay their respects have a place to come and reflect.

The park is also a beautiful picnic area for camaraderie and is home to monuments and memorials honoring and paying tribute to our Fallen Marines and Sailors of 5th Marines. The organization dedicated an Operation Iraqi Freedom Monument in 2009 and an Operation Enduring Freedom Monument in 2013. The Memorial Park is a gathering place where many memories are made, including celebrations and promotions.

Texts barriers are placed at the memorial site to commemorate 5th Marines' participation in Operation Enduring Freedom and Operation Iraqi Freedom.

BUILDING A PLACE OF HONOR FOR OUR HEROES

BY TERRY RIFKIN, CHAIRMAN OF THE BOARD AND
MEMBER OF THE ADVISORY BRIGADE, DANA POINT
5TH MARINE REGIMENT SUPPORT GROUP

As the Iraq War was heating up, many of the cities close to Camp Pendleton adopted Marine Units, Battalions and Regiments. In 2004, the City of Dana Point adopted the 5th Marine Regiment. This adoption lay dormant until late 2007 and early 2008 when it became The Dana Point 5th Marine Regiment Support Group (DP5MRSG) with a Tax Exempt 501(c)(3) Non-Profit Status.

Our heart-felt and compelling mission is to provide support and outreach for the benefit of our active-duty Marines, Sailors, our wounded warriors at Wounded Warrior Battalion— West, and families whether deployed or stateside. In accordance with this trust, with no salaries, we strive to fill in the gaps of what our Marine Corps provides and keep the morale of our brave defenders and their loved ones high. A high priority is to also pay tribute to our fallen heroes so they are "Never Forgotten."

One of DP5MRSG's early initiatives in 2008 was to establish the 5th Marines Memorial Park. It is a revered site where families, Marine Comrades-in-Arms, and those who wish to pay their respects have a place to come and reflect. The park is also a picnic area for camaraderie and is home to monuments and memorials honoring and paying tribute to our Fallen Marines and Sailors of the 5th Marine Regiment.

Then **Col. Larry D. Nicholson,** Commander of the 5th Marine Regiment and RCT-5, approached some of our founders with a vision. He drew a Texas-barrier, like ones used in Iraq and Afghanistan to shield from impact blasts, on a napkin and shared the idea to create an Operation Enduring Freedom Monument to honor and never forget those who made the ultimate sacrifice for our freedom in the Iraq War.

The Iraqi Freedom Barrier, now on display at the 5th Marines Memorial Park, has been a special place for those who wish to come and pay their respects in the presence of this beautiful memorial. At any given time we may see families of those who served in Iraq, their Marine brothers, and others who wish to pray for their loved ones at this solemn spot. With remaining funds, a beautiful bronze Boots Display is located in the 5th Marines Chow Hall in the 62 area.

By the end of 2012, 5th Marines no longer had a presence in Afghanistan and Regimental Combat Team Five (RCT-5) and other Marine units had begun the process of downsizing and transferring security over to their Afghan counterparts. Victory, however, came at a very high price and it was time to remember and pay tribute to those who made the ultimate sacrifice from the 5th Marine Regiment, Regimental Combat Team Five and other distinguished

Marine Units. To this end, all the 5th Marines Adoptive Cities; Laguna Hills, Dana Point, Rancho Santa Margarita, Costa Mesa, and San Clemente, in concert with 5th Marines, put in place a permanent Operation Enduring Freedom monument to pay proper tribute to our fallen Marines. This 7-ton granite monument was transported from sea to shining sea. Designed by Rock of Ages out of Barre, Vermont, and transported

from state to state and escorted on its 10-day journey by our esteemed Patriot Guard Riders. The OEF monument was dedicated on June 7, 2013 by **Col. Roger B. Turner** who addressed his Marines and **Gen. John F. Kelly,** the force Commander of U.S. Southern Command and Gold Star Father, who was in attendance and gave a riveting speech only moments after seeing his own son's name on the monument.

In addition, our 5th Marines wounded-in-action deserved special recognition for their personal courage shown and sacrifices made. On Feb. 22, 2017, an enduring Purple Heart monument was dedicated in the 5th Marines Memorial Park on George Washington's Birthday to serve as a symbol of the bravery of 5th Marines wounded in action. **Col. Ken R. Kassner,** then Commander of the 5th Marine Regiment, was twice wounded in Iraq in support of Operation Iraqi Freedom said it was his hope that this Purple Heart Memorial Monument be dedicated as a permanent tribute at San Mateo, Home of the 5th Marines. This monument now

serves as a symbol of the personal courage and sacrifices made in the name of freedom by all the Fighting Fifth Warriors it represents.

Our most recent collaboration has been a "Welcome Home" memorial monument to honor the 2,706 5th Marines and Sailors who lost their lives while serving in the Vietnam War. It took over four years from conception to reality to erect this outstanding monument and at long last, Memorial Day, May 28, 2018, our goal became a reality. The team faced many challenges including confirming the identification of every one of our combat KIA.

This monument stands in the 5th Marines Memorial Park today with 2,706 names, rank and KIA dates forever etched into the majestic black granite panels. It became a heart-warming experience as nearly 400 individuals, corporations, and non-profit organizations contributed to this beautiful structure. Once again, Rock of Ages fabricated the monument and three trucks transported the monument escorted by our Patriot Guard Riders.

Vietnam Memorial – Photo courtesy of Heather Bohm Tallman Photography

We reflect on the valor and sacrifices made by those 2,706 Marines and Sailors, as well as the over 14,000 Marines and Sailors from other units who died in Vietnam. These Marines and Sailors whose names are on these granite panels, raised their hands, answered the call of duty, put on a pack, traveled 10,000 miles to a distant country, pushed through rice paddies, heat, and monsoon, fought honorably and heroically to protect the ideals we hold dear as Marines and Americans. They gave all they had and all they would ever have.

It is the honor and privilege of the Dana Point 5th Marine Regiment Support Group to forever remember the brave Fighting Fifth Marines who were wounded and killed in action. We share the sorrows and scorching pain along with our Marines, Sailors, Wounded Warriors and Gold Star families as they pay tribute and honor to those they will never see again.

Helping to bring these Warriors home to the 5th Marine Regiment with these enduring tributes demonstrates our recognition of their courage and extraordinary valor in service to their country. We thank their families and friends for their sacrifice.

Terry Rifkin

U.S. Marine Corps photo by Lance Cpl. Rhita Daniel

A wreath is laid near the 5th Marines Vietnam War Memorial in the Camp San Mateo Memorial Garden on May 28, 2018. The memorial is inscribed with the names of 2,706 Marines and Sailors who gave their lives serving our great nation.

About Terry: Terry Rifkin had a private practice in Laguna Niguel as a licensed Psychotherapist and holds a Diplomate in Clinical Social Work. She is a published author and has served as a Clinical Adjunct Professor at the University of Southern California. Terry is a Charter member, Past President, and Past Director of the Monarch Beach Sunrise Rotary Club, and a sustaining Paul Harris Fellow. In 2008, Terry was selected to be the Rotary District Business Rotarian of the Year. In March of 2012, Terry was honored by Assemblywoman Diane Harkey as the 73rd Assembly District Woman of the Year. This honor was given for Terry's tireless community service and her devoted efforts with our military troops and their families. When the Dana Point 5th Marine Regiment Support Group was incorporated, she was on the inaugural board and is the only remaining Director from its origin. She served as Director of Support and Outreach between 2008-2012 and then President of the organization through the end of 2018. She is now the Chairman of the Board and a member of the Advisory Brigade.

Artist rendering courtesy of 11th Marine Ceremonial Garden Association

11TH MARINES CEREMONIAL GARDEN

The 11th Marines Ceremonial Garden Wall of Honor is still under construction, but when finished, it will recognize the brave service of all Cannon Cocker veterans along with the batteries and battalions that they served in. The 11th Marines Ceremonial Garden, located at Camp Las Pulgas, will be a serene and beautiful place for families and friends to visit their loved ones. It will be a place to reflect and remember them and a celebratory place where the 11th Marines will join together for promotions, retirements, and ceremonies to honor all "Cannon Cocker" veterans. The project is being coordinated with veterans of 11th Marines who have partnered with the Rotary Clubs of San Juan Capistrano and Camp Pendleton to raise money and complete the memorial in 2021.

'Harriers Inbound'

Col. Larry Nicholson, commander of Regimental Combat Team-5, being interviewed by Maj. Jeff Riley, a Marine historian at Camp Fallujah, Iraq, Oct. 1, 2006. Painted by Durr while on assignment for the National Museum of the Marine Corps.

'Shooter,' Gunnery Sgt. Julia Watson, assigned to 3rd Civil Affairs Group, in Fallujah, Iraq.

PAINTING HISTORY IN A COMBAT ZONE

Combat artists aim to preserve the experience and activities of military men and women through art. The works document the lives of service members in battle and in training, during humanitarian missions, and on the home front. The Marine Corps Combat Art Program traces its origins to 1942. Managed today by the National Museum of the Marine Corps, the collection has grown to include more than 9,000 works of art created by more than 350 artists.

Col. Larry Nicholson, commander of Regimental Combat Team-5, visits a local market in Fallujah, Iraq, in the summer of 2006.

Among those is Lt. Col. Alex Durr, USMC (Ret.), who covered operations in Iraq and Afghanistan in 2006. Here is a collection of some watercolors and wall art from his deployments while on assignment for the National Museum of the Marine Corps.

BY LT. COL. ALEX DURR, USMC (RET.)

In June 2006, I was mobilized for about 10 months and assigned to the Field History Branch of the National Museum of the Marine Corps and responsible for capturing images from the front lines using watercolors and other painting techniques.

As a combat artist, I was able to travel around to capture a variety of operations such as grunts in Ramadi, air wingers at Al Asad, Civil Affairs in Fallujah and then a special project assigned by then Col. Larry Nicholson, commander of Regimental Combat Team 5. I painted a large memorial on a "Texas" barrier for a local Iraqi Chief of Police who was slain.

In August of 2006, I was able to travel to Afghanistan for about a month, attached to the Marines at Bagram Air Field, that included many trips to Kabul and a night at a forward operating base (FOB) near the Pakistan border, which included a mortar attack at the beginning of a Sept. 11 remembrance ceremony!

I was back in Fallujah when I had the idea to return via the "medivac" route. I was able to depart Fallujah to Ballad, Iraq, then on to the Regional Medical Facility at Landstuhl, Germany, where I boarded a C-17 with wounded warriors on their way to Andrews Air Force Base, Maryland. I was able to travel back on the C-17 with some of the Marines whom I drew on the operating table in Fallujah, just a week earlier.

Upon returning to the 1st Marine Expeditionary Force (I MEF) at Camp Pendleton and the History Division in Quantico, I was able to work on some paintings before I was released from active duty in May 2007. I was promoted to lieutenant colonel and shortly after my return from deployment.

I was able to join a reserve unit in Fort Worth as their Air Officer and in 2010 I was mobilized for ten months with 3rd Marine Air Wing (Forward) and deployed to Camp Leatherneck, Afghanistan. The command there was very approving of me doing some art work around the base and during my travels. Many watercolors that either have been sent or will be sent to the National Museum of the Marine Corps.

Upon my return from active duty, I was able to continue my career as an airline pilot, father to two wonderful daughters and I continue painting. I get the occasional commissions, as well as do my own paintings.

My mission as a combat artist was to document through artwork, all the Marine activities in a combat zone. It's all about the young men and women who serve our country. I once accompanied Gen. James Mattis to The Basic School in Quantico, Virginia, where he addressed the new officers. I started to draw him and he stopped me and said "draw the young Marines—it's about them."

One of my personal joys was to share, or give some of the art work to those I come across. I hope my contributions to this book offers a glimpse into what life was like for our troops in Afghanistan and Iraq and honors their service and sacrifices.

Semper Fi,

Alex Durr

Lieutenant Colonel, USMCR (Ret.)

Durr painted a "Texas" barrier of a slain Iraqi police chief from Fallujah as a tribute to his efforts to work with U.S. forces in trying to build security in Anbar Province, Iraq, during the summer of 2006.

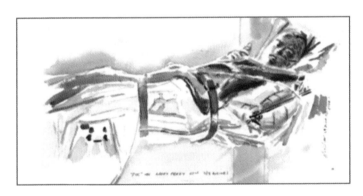

Durr was a reservist and recalled to active duty to serve as a combat artist for the National Museum of the Marine Corps (NMMC) in 2006. He painted unit logos on some of the walls and created beautiful watercolor paintings to capture the faces of Marines serving in Al Anbar Province, Iraq.

About Alex: Alex Durr currently works as an airline pilot and lives in Fort Worth, Texas. Born and raised in South Florida, he attended Florida State University and graduated in 1983 with a degree in studio art. Following graduation, he entered the U.S. Marine Corps, and he served his first nine and a half years of active duty as a pilot, flying the F-4 Phantom and F/A-18 Hornet. He retired from the U.S. Marine Corps Reserves in 2011. His assignments included a tour as a pilot, combat artist, air officer with an artillery regiment and as an operations officer with the 3rd Marine Air Wing, which included a tour in Afghanistan. As an artist, he specialized in aviation art and has works included in the permanent collection of the National Museum of the Marine Corps, National Museum of Naval Aviation and the U.S. Air Force Art collection.

CAMP PENDLETON MARINES TRANSFER SECURITY IN ANBAR PROVINCE, IRAQ

U.S. Marine Corps Maj. Gen. John F. Kelly, commander of I MEF (Forward) and Multi-National Force—West, signed the documents that transferred security of the province to the Iraqi civilian authority and to the Iraqi security forces. The ceremony was held at the Provincial Government Center in the capital city of Ramadi on Sept. 8, 2008.

Al Anbar Province Governor Ma'moon Rashid Alwani delivered a passionate speech while about 500 Anbaris attended the event that showcased the Iraqi Security Forces on parade. This was the beginning of the drawdown for all of U.S. forces in Iraq and the catalyst for ending the U.S. Marine presence in Anbar Province after more than five years of sustained combat operations in the region.

Sgt. Maj. Neil O'Connell presented a U.S. flag to the civilian leadership in Anbar Province, Iraq, during the transfer of security ceremony Sept. 8, 2008. O'Connell served as the I Marine Expeditionary Force (Forward) senior enlisted leader from 2008-2009. (Courtesy photos)

Amy Forsythe was on assignment as a Marine photographer and videographer in Anbar Province, Iraq in 2006 and 2008. Pictured here in 2006, she was covering a meeting with the local police and U.S. training teams in Ramadi, Iraq.

Helicopter Landing Zone at Camp Blue Diamond in Ramadi, Iraq, 2006.

Marines from 3rd Assault Amphibian Battalion, based at Camp Pendleton, patrol the dusty streets of Dulab, Iraq, July 17, 2006. (Photo by Sgt. Roe F. Seigle)

BOOTS ON THE GROUND IN IRAQ AND AFGHANISTAN

(Courtesy photo)

CHAPTER 4

A PLACE TO HEAL

The Wounded Warrior Battalion—West complex is named in honor of U.S. Marine Sgt. Rafael Peralta, who was mortally wounded in combat during the Second Battle of Fallujah during the Iraq War on Nov. 15, 2004.

Peralta, whose family lives in San Diego, is buried in Fort Rosecrans National Cemetery in San Diego, California. As combat operations in both Iraq and Afghanistan continued, Marines and Sailors based at Camp Pendleton needed a place to recover and rehabilitate and the center officially opened in 2010.

WARRIORS CONNECTED FOREVER

No Man Left Behind statue is placed in front of the Warrior Hope and Care Center on Camp Pendleton. The monument was created to honor those wounded in the line of duty and those who never returned home. Representing the ultimate price of battle, the spirit of brotherhood, and dedication known by service members and their families, the photograph "Hell House" and now the monument *No Man Left Behind* are iconic to our service members.

The monument was created by John Phelps, an artist, Vietnam veteran, and Gold Star Father. John's son, Lance Cpl. Chance Phelps was killed in action in Anbar Province, Iraq, in April 2004. The HBO® movie, *Taking Chance,* chronicled the

journey of a Marine officer responsible for escorting Chance's body home to his final resting place at the Dubois Cemetery in Dubois, Wyoming.

Hope For The Warriors® is the organization that coordinated and provided the monuments to the Marine Corps aboard on both Camp Lejeune and Camp Pendleton. The statue is based on a famous wartime photo by acclaimed combat photographer Lucian Read. It brings to life the iconic photo "Hell House," captured in Fallujah It depicts two Marine Corps Lance Corporals, Chris Marquez and Dane Shaffer, as they were rescuing then 1st Sgt. Bradley Kasal.

Sgt. Rafael Peralta is a Marine Corps icon, born in Mexico City, raised in South San Diego County, and valiantly died for his country in the second battle of Fallujah, Iraq in 2004. He was recommended for the Congressional Medal of Honor and was awarded the Nation's second highest combat award, the Navy Cross. Peralta led his team through three house-clearings before charging into the fourth house. After finding two rooms empty on the ground floor he opened a third door and was hit multiple times with AK-47 fire, leaving him severely wounded.

Peralta fell to the floor, moving aside to enable the Marines behind him to return fire. The insurgents threw a hand grenade at the Marines, and the two Marines with Peralta tried to get out of the room but could not. Still conscious on the floor, despite his wounds Peralta reportedly pulled the grenade under his body, absorbing most of the blast and shrapnel. He died instantly, but saved the lives of his fellow Marines. Many senior officials recommended Peralta receive the Medal of Honor for his actions, but was awarded the Navy Cross posthumously.

The Arleigh Burke-class guided-missile destroyer USS Rafael Peralta (DDG 115) was commissioned in a ceremony at Naval Air Station North Island in San Diego, California, July 27, 2017.

The naming of the ship honors Marine Corps Sgt. Rafael Peralta, who was posthumously awarded the Navy Cross for actions during Operation Iraqi Freedom.

U.S. Navy photo by Mass Communication Specialist 2nd Class Zackary Alan Landers

In November 2004, embedded photographer Lucian Read captured one of the most memorable battlefield images of the U.S. war in Iraq. The famous photograph shows a wounded and bloody 1st Sgt. Brad Kasal as he emerged from a building in Fallujah, Iraq, in 2004 supported by Marines on his left and right.

Photo by Lucian Read

The **No Man Left Behind** *statue was crafted by Wyoming artist John Phelps whose son, Marine Pvt. Chance Phelps, was killed in combat in April 2004 in Ramadi, Iraq.*

The photograph captured in 2004 would later provide inspiration to sculptor John Phelps, a Gold Star father whose son, Lance Cpl. Chance Phelps, was killed in Iraq in 2004. Versions of Phelps' sculpture, "Hell House," now stand at the entrance to Wounded Warrior Hope and Care Centers at Camp Lejeune, North Carolina, and Camp Pendleton, California.

Kasal, a first sergeant at the time, had sustained wounds from seven bullets and taken more than 43 pieces of grenade shrapnel during a firefight. He reportedly lost 60 percent of his blood by the time he emerged from the house, supported by two lance corporals, but still brandishing his sidearm and Ka-Bar knife.

In 2006, Kasal received the Navy Cross, the military's second-highest award for valor, for his heroism that day. According to his medal citation, Kasal had rolled on top of a wounded Marine to shield him, absorbing the shrapnel from an enemy grenade with his own body. Kasal retired from his post as sergeant major of the 1st Marine Expeditionary Force on May 18, 2018.

Sgt. Maj. Brad Kasal, depicted in the photo and statue, went on to serve as the I Marine Expeditionary Force senior enlisted leader from 2015 to 2018. Kasal retired from active duty in the same year.

An HBO movie in 2009, Taking Chance, *starring Kevin Bacon, told the story of returning Chance Phelps' body to his hometown for burial.*

Chance Phelps was assigned to a Camp Pendleton-based unit when he was killed in 2004. His father, John, who served as a Marine, created the No Man Left Behind *monument for Camp Pendleton and Camp Lejeune.*

by Colonel Greg Martin, USMC (Ret.)

In the years of combat operations following 9/11, "Keeping Faith with our Marines" was often cited as a priority second only to warfighting for Marine Corps leadership. One of the most tangible examples of doing this was the establishment of the Wounded Warrior Regiment in 2007 followed by Wounded Warrior Battalion—West at Camp Pendleton and a similar unit at Camp Lejeune in North Carolina.

Wounded Warrior Battalion—West was charged with taking care of the non-medical needs of our wounded, ill, and injured warriors west of the Mississippi and in the Pacific. Camp Pendleton is home to the largest number of operational forces in the entire Marine Corps and was the obvious choice for the headquarters. These units remain in operation and have grown a reputation as a model across the Department of Defense for helping our warriors go from **surviving to thriving.**

This effort has enjoyed top levels of support from Marine Corps leadership, our local communities, and many wonderful non-profit organizations that grew out of a nation-wide desire to improve the overall care of this generation. I believe that some of this is due to our national shame in the way our Vietnam veterans were treated when returning home from combat.

Three state-of-the art buildings make up what is now called the Sergeant Rafael Peralta Wounded Warrior Center at Camp Pendleton. They are the Wounded Warrior Barracks, the Warrior Hope and Care Center, and the Wounded Warrior Battalion Headquarters. In 2014, the *No Man Left Behind* statue was put into place and stands as a symbolic reminder of the sacrifices made by so many during combat operations in Iraq and Afghanistan.

The Wounded Warrior Battalion has been key in improving the lives of hundreds of our wounded,

ill, and injured moving onto productive self-sufficient lives. The battalion's programs were built around four lines of effort: mind, body, spirit, and family, with the philosophy that focused efforts on these parts of an individual's life that will present a better and brighter future for Marines and their families as they move beyond their injuries or illness.

The location of the Wounded Warrior Center was carefully selected based on the quiet and beautiful surroundings of Lake O'Neill in the heart of the base where it was envisioned that those suffering from combat related stress issues could best relax and recover.

The motto of the battalion is **Etium in Pugna** – Still in the Fight.

Col. Greg Martin

About Greg: Col. Greg Martin retired from active duty in 2019 after serving for 30 years. He's the President of Warrior Foundation Freedom Station based in San Diego, California. The Foundation enables our Nation's post 9-11 ill and injured warriors to live self-sufficient lives through programs that promote recovery, independence, and passion for the future.

Highlights of his career include tours as the Director of Operations in Baghdad, Iraq, four command tours including a Wounded Warrior Battalion, an Air Naval Gunfire Liaison Company, a Presidential Security Company, and an artillery battery. He also served overseas tours including one as an Exchange Officer to Royal Australian Army and one as the Policy Chief at U.S. Forces Korea.

Greg is from a San Diego military family and graduated from high school here. He has a great family including two grandchildren with another on the way. He holds a Masters in Executive Leadership from the University of San Diego School of Business. He also has master's degrees from the U.S. Army War College and the U.S. Marine Corps Command and Staff College, a Bachelor's degree from San Diego State University, and an Associate's degree from San Diego Mesa College. Greg enjoys outdoor sports including fishing, hunting, surfing, hiking, and mountain biking. He loves to spend time with his family and strives for a healthy work-life balance and self-improvement mentally, physically, and spiritually.

Lt. Gen. Richard Zilmer (above, third from left) and others involved in the construction and implementation cut the ribbon officially opening the center located in the Lake O'Neill area of Camp Pendleton, March 25, 2010. Col. Greg Martin, (above, far right) served as the commanding officer of Wounded Warrior Battalion until June of 2011. At that time, there were approximately 650 wounded, ill, or injured Marines assigned to the command.

This is an artist's rendering of the Wounded Warrior Campus at Camp Pendleton. The center opened March 25, 2010, and continues to serve wounded, ill and injured Marines and Sailors.

The Wounded Warrior Battalion—West was originally founded as the Camp Pendleton Wounded Warrior Center in August 2006. As combat operations in both Iraq and Afghanistan continued, the Marines and Sailors based at Camp Pendleton needed a place to recover and rehabilitate. The Wounded Warrior Complex at Camp Pendleton officially opened March 25, 2010 to serve the needs of Marines and Sailors.

The Wounded Warrior Regiment and two subordinate battalions provides leadership, accountability, and ensures compliance with laws and Department of Defense regulations related to the support, recovery, and non-medical care of combat and non-combat wounded, ill, and injured (WII) Marines and Sailors attached to Marine units, and their family members in order to maximize their recovery as they return to duty or transition to civilian life.

CHAPTER 5

CAMP PENDLETON DOGS OF WAR

The base's canine kennel complex, known as Camp Cann, is named after Cann, a 23-year-old from Destin, Florida. Cann was based at Camp Pendleton, California, and the first dog handler killed in action since Vietnam. U.S. Marine Sgt. Adam Cann was killed by an explosion while on patrol in Ramadi, Iraq, on Jan. 5, 2006.

The memorial is made from a barrier "T-Wall" that was originally painted at Camp Fallujah, Iraq. The barrier depicts Cann with his military working dog and has the inscription "Dogs of War" painted on the left. When Marines left Camp Fallujah, the barrier wall was brought back to Camp Pendleton and placed at the entrance to the kennel complex located near the San Luis Rey gate.

Sgt. Adam Cann with his military working dog, Bruno. Cann was killed on Jan. 5, 2006 and he's buried at Section 60 at Arlington National Cemetery. (Courtesy photo)

K-9 HILL — 'FROM A FEW OF THE FINEST, TO THE FINEST OF THE FEW'

Tucked away towards the south side of Camp Pendleton, California, are eight crosses bearing the names of U.S. Marines killed in the line of duty while serving as military dog handlers in Iraq and Afghanistan. Each cross bears their names and a photo, along with American flags at the base of the cross. This memorial was established in 2017 by families of the fallen.

IN MEMORY OF

Sgt. Adam L. Cann

Sgt. Christopher M. Wrinkle

Cpl. Max W. Donahue

Cpl. Dustin J. Lee

Staff Sgt. Christopher Diaz

Cpl. Keaton G. Coffey

Sgt. Joshua R. Ashley

Cpl. David M. Sonka

A 6-foot granite memorial sits at the military working dog kennel complex at Camp Pendleton, California. The memorial is dedicated to the U.S. Marine Corps working dogs and was spearheaded by the efforts of Kyle Cabodi, Eagle Scout from Boy Scouts of America, Troop 737. The memorial was placed and dedicated in August 2003.

A plaque was placed at the site of the military working dog handlers crosses on Camp Pendleton, California. The plaque reads: "From a few of the finest, to the finest of the few. This Memorial is dedicated to the Marine Military Working Dog Handlers who were killed in Iraq and Afghanistan. We honor the memory of the these Marines. Their Service and Sacrifice will Never be Forgotten." Dedicated April 1, 2016

A LEGACY REBORN

BY MIKE DOWLING, U.S. MARINE VETERAN AND AUTHOR OF *SERGEANT REX: THE UNBREAKABLE BOND BETWEEN A MARINE AND HIS MILITARY WORKING DOG*

Marine Corps military working dog teams at Camp Pendleton have a storied history dating back to the beginning of the war dog program in WWII. The Marine war dog platoons of WWII initially trained in Camp Lejeune and then were sent by railroad to Camp Pendleton for advanced training and deployment readiness.

Deploying from Camp Pendleton, they served in the South Pacific where they earned respect and admiration from the Marine infantry units they were attached to. Initially thought of as unproven experimental units, war dog teams distinguished themselves as vital assets on the battlefield and began a legacy and inspiration for all future Marine dog teams.

However, after Vietnam, the need for war dog teams diminished and their purpose evolved from battlefield services as sentry dogs, scout dogs, and messenger dogs, to providing garrison duties. They no longer focused on training for combat as war dogs, instead they specialized in providing security to military bases and became known as military working dogs.

"The events of September 11th, 2001 changed everything."

Buildup for war in Afghanistan and Iraq were happening and it was unclear what use, if any, dogs would have in the upcoming conflicts, but one thing was clear, they were not ready or prepared for today's combat environments.

I left for Marine Corps boot camp in mid-August 2001 and the events of 9/11 happened when I was there. While the world was rapidly changing, I was exactly where I wanted to be, training to be a Marine. I had enlisted on an open contract, meaning I left my fate to the Marine Corps to choose my military occupational specialty for me, a move that comes with great risk as they can assign me to any job they wanted to.

After 9/11 there was talk of war on the horizon which made me feel for sure I would become infantry. Instead, I was selected to become a military policeman, a job that had never crossed my mind. While I was happy to be a Marine, I wasn't sure if I would be happy being an MP, that is until I learned that MP's can be selected to become military working dog handlers.

Back in the early 2000s, it was not widely known that dogs were utilized in the military and I had never known being a dog handler was even an option. I grew up with a huge affinity for dogs thanks to my family fostering and training guide dogs for the blind as well as having our own pet dogs. I knew without a doubt that I would love being a handler the second I learned of it, felt I had found my calling, and I would do whatever it took to become one.

Living the Dream

But becoming a military working dog handler is very difficult since each dog is incredibly valuable and you are responsible for it's well being. A great deal of initiative and personal accountability is required so it is a great honor to be selected as a handler. I had a laser focus and my determination would pay off as I would become the honor graduate of my military police class and achieved my goal of being selected as a handler. After completing the military working dog handler's course at Lackland Air Force Base, I got assigned to the Camp Pendleton Military Working Dog section in the spring of 2002.

I felt like I was living the dream. I had enlisted in the Marines during peacetime wanting a challenge, sense of purpose, and to serve my country. By the time I finished all my initial training and arrived to Camp Pendleton, our country was at war and through a combination of luck, hard work, and faith that I was making the right decisions, I ended up in what I thought was the best possible job for me assigned to what I was being told by my dog handler instructors was the best K-9 unit in the Marine Corps.

> *"I was loving life because the Camp Pendleton K-9 unit was exactly the kind of unit I wanted to be a part of..."*

They took great pride in being Marines and even more in being the best dog teams they could be. They were great dog trainers, loved to train hard, and every day was challenging and exciting because we all knew, with the wars beginning, that dogs could be utilized to serve in combat once again. It felt like there was no room for error and training took on more importance than ever.

Turmoil at the Kennels

Unfortunately, as incredible as that K-9 unit was, it turned out there was an undercover NCIS investigation being conducted on that unit. To this day I don't know all the details, but before I got assigned there, some handlers in that unit allegedly had done something illegal and NCIS found out about it and began an investigation that lasted several months. Eventually, instead of holding the handlers they allege did illegal behavior, they held the entire unit accountable and every handler in that unit, myself included, was charged with various disciplinary actions in the fall of 2002.

Ultimately, I was exonerated of everything and allowed to go back to being a handler. The rest of the handlers in that unit received some type of disciplinary decision and many were either kicked out of the K-9 section or kicked out of the Marines. Out of the 21 handlers in the unit, I was one of three Marines that were allowed to go back to being a handler.

The timing of all this was terrible. We had great unit cohesion and we were training hard knowing dog teams were going to be needed for the upcoming war efforts. It all came crashing down. All my handler friends were now kicked out of K-9, their mentorship and expert dog training skills gone, and to make matters worse, every amazing military working dog on that base was no longer certified and allowed to work in the military.

I went from feeling I was in the best possible position I could be in as a Marine dog handler, having access to great trainers, great Marines, and great dogs, to losing them all. It was a real low point for me as a young Marine. The Camp Pendleton K-9 unit went from being known as an elite and well respected K-9 unit to now having to be completely rebuilt with new dogs and new handlers, overnight.

Rebuilding and Forming a Great Team

So the rebuilding began in the fall of 2002 as new handlers and dogs were getting assigned to Camp Pendleton. The beginning of the new K-9 unit started with myself along with handlers Lance Cpl. Jason Cannon, Lance Cpl. Adam Cann, Lance Cpl. Mario Cardenas, Sgt. Vincent Amato, and Kennel Master Staff Sgt. Greg Massey. We also got new dogs starting with MWD Rex (assigned to me), MWD Robby (assigned to Cannon), MWD Rokka (assigned to Cardenas), and MWD Bruno (assigned to Cann).

We didn't have time to dwell on what had happened to the previous unit and the gossip surrounding it. We banded together and became determined to build the K-9 unit back to being respected and a unit known for having high expectations and training hard. In that transition, we all felt the pressure of not just rebuilding but training for what inevitably was to come, combat operations. Unfortunately, as determined as we were, we admittedly had little idea of what we would expect to encounter in Afghanistan or Iraq or how to train for it.

Nonetheless, we trained and trained and trained. We put all our focus on being better handlers, improving our dogs, and being in the best physical shape of our lives so that we felt prepared for whatever unknowns would come. Through that process, we felt all of our dogs were rapidly becoming great, except for one, MWD Bruno who was assigned to Lance Cpl. Adam Cann.

Bruno's slow development was not a knock on Adam's abilities as a handler. By every measure, Adam was a great Marine, a great friend, and he absolutely loved being a handler. He came to Camp Pendleton after having already served a year in Japan and had experience. Some dogs simply don't come to the fleet with the same amount of drive and ability to pick up training as quickly as others do.

Since the unit was rebuilding, getting new handlers and new dogs regularly, Adam could have easily asked to be reassigned to another new dog to work with that showed more promise since he had seniority over the new handlers that were arriving. Instead, he accepted the challenge of turning Bruno into a great working dog, and was determined to get the best out of him.

Ready for Combat Deployments

By the time dog teams were asked to deploy into combat operations in the spring of 2004, the Camp Pendleton K-9 unit had almost been rebuilt back to its original capacity of dogs and handlers as it previously had. We also had some great certified dog teams by then who were eager to have their abilities put to the test down range. Myself with MWD Rex, Cannon with MWD Robby, and even MWD Bruno had finally come around to becoming a great dog. Bruno, thanks to Adam, became an example of a dog that through proper training, patience, and determination, even dogs who showed slow progress could become great with the right handler.

In the spring of 2004, all West Coast Marine Corps bases were tasked with sending dog teams to Iraq in support of combat operations for the first time. Rex and I would be on this first deployment from the Camp Pendleton K-9 section, but Jason and Adam, along with their MWD's, were just as eager and ready to have deployed. Each west coast base designated one or two MWD teams and, just like the war dog platoons of WWII, they all came to Camp Pendleton for deployment readiness training.

We did not have any combat experienced handlers or trainers so we did the best we could at training for what we thought we would encounter. We got the dogs acclimated to a lot of gunfire, loud noises, and distractions. Our primary focus, however, would be explosives detection training knowing that the number one

threat has become improvised explosive devices (IED's). We had no idea where in Iraq we would be stationed, what units we would work with, or what kinds of missions, if any, we would go on. All we knew is that we felt like we trained hard and were as best prepared as we could be.

Surviving the "Triangle of Death"

When we got to Iraq in spring 2004, all the dog teams were assigned to Marine units across the country and Rex and I would be attached to 2nd Battalion, 2nd Marines who were tasked with operating in the ominous area known as the "Triangle of Death." An area so dangerous that, by the end of the seven month deployment, 2/2 had suffered six killed in action (KIA) and over 150 wounded.

It was a baptism by fire experience for all dog teams. None of us had trained with infantry units prior to deployment, and now here we are leading infantry patrols and missions with our dogs out in front detecting explosives and clearing the way forward. Once again, dog teams were an experimental unit just like the WWII dog teams from before. Working in a new and unforgiving environment with excruciating heat, freezing cold, and leading infantry Marines they had never met or trained with prior to deploying.

Thankfully, all the dog teams from that first deployment survived and, once again, distinguished themselves from unproven units to becoming critical assets in warfare. All the teams did exceptionally well and helped spearhead new training tactics, gear and developed standard operating procedures.

While I returned with Rex, other Camp Pendleton handlers like Jason and Adam, got to deploy with their military working dogs. The Camp Pendleton K-9 team had come a long way from having to rebuild from the ground up to becoming a thriving, hard-working unit once again, regularly deploying dog teams to support combat operations. And for the first time in decades it had added something to the unit, dogs and handlers with combat experience.

Danger Everywhere

Searching for explosives is incredibly dangerous, yet handlers were surprisingly surviving their deployments and coming home relatively unscathed. Unfortunately, the inevitable was to come.

> *"On Jan. 5, 2006, Sgt. Adam Cann, from the Camp Pendleton K-9 section, was the first dog handler to be killed in combat action since the Vietnam war."*

He had already survived one deployment with MWD Bruno to Iraq and they were now on their second. He was killed in Ramadi, Iraq, by a suicide bomber.

Adam and Bruno were one of three dog teams on that day's mission. They were being a deterrent and maintaining security for Iraqi civilians who were applying to join the local police. As Adam and Bruno walked along the line of civilians that were hoping to become police, Bruno alerted on an individual standing in line.

The bomber, underneath his clothing, was wearing a vest with explosives attached which he detonated without hesitation once he saw Bruno alert. Standing right next to the bomber, Adam died, along with many Iraqi civilians, but MWD Bruno, who Adam worked so hard to become a great working dog, had survived. If Bruno had not done his job, the bomber would have made it inside the building where he could have done a massive amount of damage.

Dog Handler Down

Adam's death sent a shockwave through the military K-9 community. He had done everything right. He had trained hard and made Bruno a great dog - they were already a combat experienced dog team. They were prepared, confident, and had trust in each other's abilities. Adam died doing what he loved most and what he was great at, being a Marine Corps military working dog handler.

Adam's contributions in helping rebuild the Camp Pendleton K-9 unit, his combat operations, and setting the best examples of leadership and hard work are legendary. He took so much pride in being a Marine K-9 handler that he took an old Camp Pendleton K-9 unit sign that had fallen into disrepair and led a team of handlers to repaint and repair it to look brand new. That sign is the first sign you see when entering the Camp Pendleton K-9 section today. He also got a "Dogs of War" tattoo to represent his combat experience as a K-9 handler. A tattoo many Camp Pendleton handlers, including myself, were inspired to get, following his lead.

Sgt. Adam Cann and his military working dog Bruno at Camp Pendleton.

Camp Pendleton War Dogs sign was unveiled on July 20, 2013.

Honoring His Memory

After his death, a memorial of him was created on a blast wall in Camp Fallujah by the dog teams that were serving there. That wall was shipped back to the states when the base closed down and now sits in front of the Camp Pendleton K-9 unit. An image of him and MWD Bruno, along with his "Dogs of War" tattoo design are on the wall.

Camp Pendleton has continued to send incredible dog teams down range to support combat operations over the years, and handlers from there have gone on to earn awards, combat valor medals, and some, like Adam, have paid the ultimate sacrifice. Those handlers build on a legacy started by the original war dog teams of WWII.

"Camp Pendleton K-9 is hallowed ground for all handlers that pick up a leash there."

Personally, I set out to simply have a challenge in life when I joined the Marines. Enlisting during peacetime and on an open contract. I never would have imagined that I would be so lucky to work in what is one of the greatest jobs there is in the military, assigned to a historic unit, have to fight to stay there, help to rebuild it, and then deploy to perform one of the most dangerous jobs in combat with my dog, MWD Rex. Serving as a dog handler at Camp Pendleton was the greatest honor of my life. I never took it for granted, and I know Adam would say the same.

Semper K-9,
Sgt. Mike Dowling
Handler of MWD Rex E168

About Mike: Mike Dowling served in the U.S. Marine Corps as a military working dog handler at Camp Pendleton from 2002 to 2005 and deployed in support of Operation Iraqi Freedom in 2004 with his MWD Rex E168. They were attached to 2nd Battalion, 2nd Marines working in the Iraq cities of Mahmudiyah, Kharma, Zaidan, and Fallujah. He is author of the book *Sergeant Rex: The Unbreakable Bond Between A Marine and His Military Working Dog* which is a memoir of his service as a K-9 handler. From 2008-2010 he was mobilized from the reserves to work with the Wounded Warrior Battalion—West and Naval Medical Center in San Diego where he assisted wounded warriors throughout their rehabilitation after suffering combat injuries. He now lives in Los Angeles and works as a producer on a wide range of productions including the Netflix Medal of Honor docuseries. He has been a dedicated veterans' advocate and been awarded Veteran of the Year title for California's 46th District. Learn more: www.officialmikedowling.com

Major Megan Malia McClung
April 14th, 1972 - December 6th, 2006
Semper Fidelis

CHAPTER 6

"BE BOLD. BE BRIEF. BE GONE."

Maj. Megan M. McClung was the first female Marine officer to be killed in Operation Iraqi Freedom, as well as the first female graduate of the United States Naval Academy to be killed in action since the school was founded in 1845. She coined the phrase "Be bold. Be brief. Be gone." as part of media training and preparation she provided as a public affairs officer.

McClung was 34 at the time of her death and was serving as a media relations officer assigned to the 1st Marine Expeditionary Force (Forward) when a roadside bomb killed her instantly in Ramadi, Iraq, Dec. 6, 2006. She and two other service members assigned the Army's Brigade Combat Team, Capt. Travis Patriquin and Spec. Vincent Pomante, III, were also killed.

The vehicle convoy McClung had been riding in was escorting *Newsweek* journalists when an improvised explosive device struck their vehicle. The *Newsweek* journalists were in another vehicle and escaped without injury. McClung had been escorting retired Marine Lt. Col. Oliver North (Ret.) and a *Fox News Channel* camera crew earlier in the day—and were devastated when they learned the news of the attack.

The inscription on Maj. Megan McClung's headstone located in Section 60 at Arlington National Cemetery in Washington, D.C., includes her mantra "Be Bold. Be Brief. Be Gone."

Former colleague and classmate from their time at the Defense Information School, Col. Riccoh Player wrote in an email, "Megan served with the mindset of running to the sound of battle, not away from it. She accepted every mission, every billet, every challenge with vigor, creative abandon and a find-a-way-to-make-a-way ethos."

Player, the I MEF deputy PAO during the 2006 deployment, had known McClung for many years and was devastated upon learning the news of her death that day from the director of public affairs for I MEF, Lt. Col. Bryan Salas.

Megan was promoted to the rank of major by Col. Bryan Salas (right) and then, Maj. Riccoh Player (left) at Camp Fallujah in the Spring of 2006.

Salas, who retired as a colonel a few years ago, now works as the Deputy Chief of Staff for the Customer Service and Public Engagement Directorate at U.S. Citizenship and Immigration Services for the Department of Homeland Security.

Salas had also known and worked with McClung at various times during their careers and had recruited her to deploy with him and the I MEF team as the Media Relations Officer in Anbar Province. Little did he know, or could have imagined, that a member of his team would fall victim to the violence that was mounting in the region.

I MEF (Forward) Public Affairs Office at Camp Fallujah, April 2006. Megan McClung (first row, far left) and Amy Forsythe, (first row, far right) served togther in 1995 and again during their deployment to Iraq in 2006.

Deployment day at Camp Pendleton. McClung and fellow Marines pose for a photo as they prepare to load the buses at Camp Del Mar near the I MEF headquarters at Camp Del Mar. I MEF deployed in mid-February in 2006 for a yearlong deployment to Anbar Province, Iraq.

Lynn Kinney (left), Megan McClung (center) and Amy Forsythe (right), the author, served together during their deployment to Camp Fallujah, Iraq in 2006. They were assigned to the Camp Pendleton-based I Marine Expeditionary Force (Forward) Public Affairs Office. This photo was taken at Camp Fallujah in April 2006. McClung was killed by an IED in Ramadi, Iraq, Dec. 6, 2006. Kinney, now a master sergeant, serves at Camp Lejeune, North Carolina.

Sheik Abdul-Sattar Abu Risha Sattar (left) and Megan McClung (right) worked together before her death in December 2006. Sheik Sattar was the founder of the Anbar Awakening movement in late 2006 that transformed Al Anbar Province from the Triangle of Death in 2006 to a triumph over Al Qaeda in 2007. He was assassinated near his home in Ramadi, Iraq, Sept. 13, 2007. (Courtesy photo)

In Megan's honor, her image was placed on the side of a bus supporting the non-profit organization "Carry the Load" that made its way across the nation in 2021. Carry the Load was founded by veteran U.S. Navy SEALs, Clint Bruce and Stephen Holley, and started as a mission to restore the true meaning of Memorial Day. (Courtesy photo)

Master Sgt. Willie Ellerbrock, pays his respects at the memorial service for Megan at the Chapel of Hope at Camp Fallujah in Anbar Province, Iraq, just days after her death in December 2006. (U.S. Marine Corps photo by Lynn Kinney)

A ROCK TO REMEMBER

by Colonel Bryan Salas, USMC (Ret.)

Prior to deploying to Iraq in early 2006, the public affairs headquarters team would hold unit physical fitness training at sunrise just outside our office on the main side of Camp Pendleton. Once a week, we would run a ridgeline that bifurcated the base from the airfield. It was a beautiful run. The undulating course would switch from tarmac to gravel. Hares and coyotes would scatter before us as we ran.

The licorice aroma of sage was wonderful in the cool air of the morning desert. The runs would be an individual effort so Megan would be up front way ahead of the rest of us. She ran effortlessly up the ridges, her red ponytail flagging in her stride. Master Sgt. Willie Ellerbrock and I would normally be towards the end of the group.

As we climbed the ridge, there was a high spot on the trail at which Willie and I would pause to gaze down at the mainside of Camp Pendleton. It was a beautiful spot. I remember turning to Willie and said, "If I ever die, bury me here. Then I could oversee the Camp Pendleton Public Affairs Office for all eternity."

After we returned from Iraq, I knew we should do something to remember Megan – and I could not get that spot out of my mind. The Marine Corps would never allow a formal memorial or statue on USMC property for Megan – regardless of how wonderful a person she was. There are many posthumous valor recipients without an individual memorial. So we'd have to make it an unofficial, discreet, and understated memorial in a semi-private place.

So I pulled a small boulder from the ranch of a Marine friend in the mountains above Camp Pendleton in Fallbrook. I took it to a memorial stone engraver to have Megan's information carved onto it's natural face, and drove it up to that spot Willie and I had paused at two years prior.

Once in place, I recall holding a formation run for the entire office of new Marines, and recently returned Iraq veterans, to honor Megan at her stone. Although a blur because of the emotion, there was testament of how tremendous a Marine and wonderful a person Megan was. I think we also talked about ensuring everyone was first and foremost prepared for the rigors of combat – some there would be deploying in a year's time back to Iraq.

I was pleasantly surprised to see how over the years Megan's friends would visit the memorial to reflect on her life. Some would leave small pebbles as evidence of their visit. More importantly, Megan has other monuments.

Most compelling are the living memorials: young women with Megan as their namesake.

Semper Fidelis,

A memorial rock was placed on one of Megan's favorite running trails on Camp Pendleton. Pictured from left to right: Lynn Kinney, Willie Ellerbrock, Amy Forsythe (author), and Sean McGinty, who were all serving with Megan when she was killed in Ramadi, Iraq, in December 2006.

About Bryan: Bryan Salas retired as a colonel a few years ago and now works as the Deputy Chief of Staff for the Customer Service and Public Engagement Directorate at U.S. Citizenship and Immigration Services for the Department of Homeland Security. Salas had also known and worked with McClung at various times during their careers and had recruited her to deploy with him and the I MEF (Forward) team as the Media Relations Officer in Anbar Province.

1ST RECONNAISSANCE BATTALION UNIT HISTORY

"SWIFT, SILENT, DEADLY"

1st Reconnaissance Battalion (abbreviated as 1st Recon Bn) is a reconnaissance battalion in the U.S. Marine Corps. It falls under the command of the 1st Marine Division and the I Marine Expeditionary Force (I MEF). 1st Recon Battalion was reactivated on July 5, 2000, as part of Marine Corps Commandant General James L. Jones' mission to revitalize Marine Corps reconnaissance.

INVASION OF IRAQ

In January 2003, the battalion deployed to Kuwait in support of Operation Enduring Freedom. The 1st Reconnaissance Battalion participated in the 2003 invasion of Iraq from March 2003 to June 2003. The battalion redeployed to Iraq for Operation Iraqi Freedom from February 2004 to October 2004, where it took part in Operation Vigilant Resolve; September 2005 to April 2006, March 2007 to October 2007, and October 2008 to April 2009.

In January 2006, the 1st Reconnaissance Battalion was in the national news for leading Operation Green Trident, which discovered over ten metric tons of insurgent munitions, hidden in caches throughout a large area south of Fallujah in the Euphrates River Valley. Marines of 1st Recon told military reporters that about 90 percent of their time in Operation Iraqi Freedom was spent in mounted patrols, using their Humvees.

OPERATION ENDURING FREEDOM: AFGHANISTAN

Elements of 1st Recon were also deployed to Helmand Province, Afghanistan in 2010 where they produced 300+ enemy KIA, did not lose a single man in their seven-month deployment and was regarded as "The deadliest battalion in Afghanistan right now" by then Lt. Gen. James Mattis.

The unit conducted a battalion-sized helicopter insert into the area of Trek Nawa, operating for 32 days straight, away from friendly lines, during that period there was contact with Taliban forces for 28 of those days using tactics and offensive action that stunned the local enemy forces. Following the missions in Trek Nawa and surrounding areas, the battalion deployed two companies to the Upper Sangin River Valley.

DEDICATED TO THE MEN OF
1ST RECONNAISSANCE BN
"Some gave all and all gave some."
"Operation Iraqi Freedom"

KIA
Capt Brent Morel
Sgt Nick Walsh

WIA

GySgt Buck Doyle   Sgt Dan Eckardt
GySgt Dave Lynn   Sgt Steve Patrick
SSgt Chuck Graves   Cpl Evan Stafford
Sgt Eric Kocher   Cpl Aaron Mazon
Sgt James E. Wright   Cpl Tony Miele
Sgt Mike Musick   Cpl Alex MacCammond
Sgt Caleb Hohman   Cpl Amish Smith
Sgt Jim Piepgrass   Cpl Casey Vague
Sgt John Bottema   Cpl Josh Murray
Sgt Ross Mcfadden

THE PADDLES OF 1ST RECONNAISSANCE BATTALION

HONORING THEIR LEGACY

Numerous wrapped paddles line the walls of the headquarters building and serve as a reminder of those who made the ultimate sacrifice. Each paddle is uniquely different with intricate wrap designs that are adorned with the name of the fallen inscribed on the placard and their 'ribbon rack' placed on the center of the flat part of the paddle.

The true history of giving paddles away as gifts was recently revealed by Lt. Col. Byron Owen. He researched the topic and wrote an article that was published in *The Havok Journal* in October 2021. Owen learned through a lot of research and several interviews that in 1974 a Recon Marine named Sgt. Armando Alonso took an old paddle from the boat locker, decorated it, and presented it to one of his teammates in appreciation of his hard work. Reconnaissance Marines and Marine Raiders have been decorating paddles as going-away gifts ever since.

The tradition of designing paddles has evolved over the years. Most paddles have the unit logo either laser engraved or painted on it, the handles are wrapped with 550 cord, the Operators badges and/or awards are attached and there's usually a plaque with the dates and a personal message. There are usually unit members that are known for their expert wrapping skills who wind up creating the units' paddles.

On the reverse side of the paddle, unit members write messages and sign their names. Paddles are a sacred piece of memorabilia for the Recon community. So, next time you see a paddle hanging on a wall, take some time to admire what goes into them.

TO:
CALEB MEDLEY
"SMEDLEY"

FROM THE SAVAGES OF
1ST FORCE RECONNAISSANCE CO
INSERT: DECEMBER 1985 EXTRACT: FEBRUARY 2013
"NO WAY BRO? YA WANT TO WORKOUT?"
"HEYYYY GAYBOY!"
"YOU KNOW WHAT I LOVE? METH"
FAIR WINDS AND FOLLOWING SEAS

Maj Kevin M. Shea
Insert: 19660914
Extract: 20040914

Kevin led by example and
always took time to listen to his Marines.

The Marine Corps and America
is a lesser place for his passing.

Fair winds and following seas, Brother Recon.

ALL IT TAKES IS ALL YOU GOT

by Master Sgt. Robert Blanton, USMC (Ret.)

"Your first duty station is something you never forget"

New to the military, I was lucky to get stationed on Camp Pendleton as a young infantry Marine. The sights, the smells, the memories. The good times and some bad, Camp Pendleton will always hold a special place in my heart.

We sometimes spend so much time thinking about the future, that we forget to live in the moment. The times that sucked the most . . . always make the best stories, so when people are recalling memories about the worst times, make sure you aren't the reason why it sucked!

Pendleton is also rich in history and while they are doing away with some of the older buildings, I always enjoyed walking into one, and imagining what it was like when some of our brothers and sisters walked into it decades ago? Embrace that history!

Honoring those who have gone before us

The Marines have done a fantastic job of creating memorials and monuments at the top of many peaks on Camp Pendleton. Next time you visit, read the names and say them out loud. Look those names up when you get home, and learn about them. Those are our brothers and sisters that we must remember.

If those hills and waves could talk, what would they say?

They would tell stories of Marines and Corpsmen persevering through adversity, coming together as a team to accomplish the mission, and overcoming all obstacles. They would also tell stories of absolute shenanigans and the laughter that ensued either during, or after no one died.

Reflections on Staff Sgt. Christopher Antonik and the saying "All it takes, is all you got"

Chris Antonik was killed in action in 2010 and he had a saying . . . "All it takes is all you got." This saying embodies what it means to give it your all. After 21 years as a Reconnaissance Marine, with many of those years being an instructor, you see those who give it their all undoubtedly, compared to those who want you to think they're giving it their all. Being retired for close to a decade now, the thing I miss the most about the Marines, is the people I served with. I miss the ones who never left doubt about their commitment to the success of what they were doing, because personally failing is letting others down.

The perfect place to train hard and play hard

Few places exist like Camp Pendleton. The ability to come from ship to shore, patrol to a training area, conduct live fire operations with close air support and explosives, then extract by a dozen different methods, makes Camp Pendleton an exceptional training base. Adding to that, the civilians who keep Camp Pendleton operating to support the service members and the excellent support from the surrounding communities, makes Camp Pendleton one of the best places to be stationed in the U.S.

Robert Blanton

Lt. Gen. Richard C. Zilmer, the commanding general of III Marine Expeditionary Force, pins the Silver Star on Gunnery Sgt. Robert Blanton during a ceremony on Camp Schwab on Jan. 8, 2009. (Courtesy photos)

About Robert: Robert Blanton is a retired U.S. Marine who served three tours of duty in Iraq. He smashed a 7-ton through the wall of an enemy infested house in Iraq, used his rifle and pistol at close quarters to recover a wounded teammate trapped inside, then blew the house up with a bomb from aircraft overhead. For his bold actions, he was awarded the Silver Star in 2009.

Blanton now serves as the CEO of Warfighter Made, based in Temecula, California, which has been supporting combat wounded veterans and their families by adapting and customizing combat wounded veterans' vehicles, so they can continue doing the things they enjoy, while their vehicle reflects their individual personality. They also provide "Camaraderie Therapy" in their 4,000 sq ft facility, by inviting all vets, from all branches, and all eras, to hang out with other veterans building projects for combat wounded amputees, maintaining therapy vehicles or simply socializing with men and women who've had similar experiences.

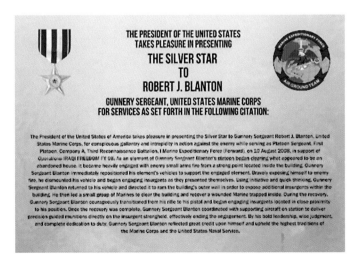

THE PRESIDENT OF THE UNITED STATES
TAKES PLEASURE IN PRESENTING

THE SILVER STAR
TO
ROBERT J. BLANTON

GUNNERY SERGEANT, UNITED STATES MARINE CORPS
FOR SERVICES AS SET FORTH IN THE FOLLOWING CITATION:

THE PURPLE FOXES: A TRIBUTE TO MORPHINE 1-2

The names of five Marines and two Sailors are painted on the CH-46 airframe that's stationary in front of the squadron's hangar on Marine Corps Air Station Camp Pendleton. Their CH-46 was shot down while flying a casualty evacuation mission in Anbar Province, Iraq on Feb. 7, 2007. Call sign MORPHINE 1-2, was flying below the clouds at about 1,500 feet above the ground and had picked up its three wounded and transported them to a hospital when they got called back to pick up and transport urgently needed blood to another location.

Those onboard MORPHINE 1-2:

Capt. Jennifer J. Harris, of Swampscott, MA

1st Lt. Jared M. Landaker, of Big Bear City, CA

Sgt. Travis D. Pfister, of Richland, WA

Sgt. James R. Tijerina, of Beasley, TX

Aside from the four Purple Fox Marines, there were two Navy Corpsman killed: Hospital Corpsman **3rd Class Manual Ruiz,** of Federalsburg, Maryland and Hospital Corpsman **1st Class Gilbert Minjares Jr.,** of El Paso, Texas.

A Marine from a different helicopter-squadron, **Cpl. Thomas E. Saba,** of Toms River, New Jersey, also was killed.

The Purple Foxes were flying CH-46 helicopters in Iraq, shown here. The squadron deployed five times in support of Operation Iraqi Freedom. (Courtesy photo)

Marine Medium Tiltrotor Squadron 364 VMM-364) is a U.S. Marine Corps medium-lift tiltrotor squadron consisting of MV-22B Ospreys. The squadron, known as the "Purple Foxes," is based at Marine Corps Air Station Camp Pendleton, California and falls under the command of Marine Aircraft Group 39 (MAG-39) and the 3rd Marine Aircraft Wing (3rd MAW).

VMM-364, formally HMM-364, has a long and proud history of flying into hot landing zones to pick up the wounded and earned the phrase, "GIVE A SHIT" during operations in Vietnam. The Purple Foxes have continued their tradition of having U.S. Navy Corpsmen on board for casualty evacuation missions.

TRAVIS MANION
KIA 4-29-07, AL ANBAR, IRAQ

CHANCE PHELPS
KIA 4-9-04, RAMADI, IRAQ

JOSEPH ELLIS
KIA 2-7-07, AL ANBAR, IRAQ

MEGAN MCCLUNG
KIA 12-6-06, RAMADI, IRAQ

HONOR

DOUGLAS ZEMBIEC
KIA 5-11-07, BAGHDAD, IRAQ

ROBERT COTTLE
KIA 3-24-10, MARJAH, AFGHANISTAN

CHRISTOPHER ANTONIK
KIA 7-11-10, HELMAND, AFGHANISTAN

RICARDO CROCKER
KIA 5-26-05, HADITHA, IRAQ

THE WALL OF HONOR SHOWCASES U.S. MARINES WHO MADE THE ULTIMATE SACRIFICE IN AFGHANISTAN OR IRAQ, WHERE DANGER WAS EVERYWHERE AND THE ENEMY DIDN'T DISCRIMINATE BASED ON JOB, GENDER, OR RANK. EACH MARINE HAD TIES TO CAMP PENDLETON AND BECAME THE INSPIRATION FOR THIS BOOK. THEIR BIOGRAPHIES ARE LISTED BELOW, BUT NO WORDS CAN COMPLETELY DESCRIBE THE VOID THEY'VE LEFT IN THE HEARTS OF THEIR FELLOW MARINES, FRIENDS AND FAMILY MEMBERS.

First Lieutenant Travis L. Manion graduated from the United States Naval Academy and was commissioned a Second Lieutenant in the United States Marine Corps in 2004. He was from Doylestown, Pennsylvania, and died April 29, 2007, at the age of 26 while conducting combat operations in Al Anbar province, Iraq. Manion was assigned to 1st Reconnaissance Battalion, 1st Marine Division, I Marine Expeditionary Force, Camp Pendleton, California.

Manion was born in Camp Lejeune, North Carolina, to an active duty Marine family. After settling in Doylestown, Pennsylvania, Travis went on to LaSalle College High School where his strong leadership qualities set him apart both athletically and academically. He was an all-league standout in wrestling, football and lacrosse, a member of five championship teams, and an All-American wrestler.

Travis was best known as a motivating and popular figure to his classmates. It was for these traits that Travis was awarded the Hal Selvey, Jr. Memorial Award for Unselfish Dedication and Leadership. This combination of leadership, athleticism, and academic achievement opened the door to his appointment to the United States Naval Academy.

Travis made the ultimate sacrifice in Al Anbar province Iraq in December 2006. He, his fellow Marines, and Iraqi Army counterparts were ambushed while searching a suspected insurgent house. Manion led the counterattack against the enemy forces. He was fatally wounded by an enemy sniper while aiding and drawing fire away from his wounded comrades. His selfless actions allowed every member of his patrol to survive.

For his actions, Travis was awarded the Silver Star and Bronze Star with Valor. His legacy continues to grow through the work of the Travis Manion Foundation, inspiring people to make an impact by serving others. Manion is buried in Section 60 at Arlington National Cemetery.

Lance Corporal Chance Russell Phelps was serving with 2nd Platoon, Battery L, 3rd Battalion, 11th Marine Regiment (3/11), 1st Marine Division, I Marine Expeditionary Force, during Operation Iraqi Freedom when he was killed in Iraq as the convoy he was escorting came under heavy fire. His story is the subject of an HBO® movie, *Taking Chance*, starring Kevin Bacon. Phelps was born in Riverton, Wyoming, moved to Craig, Colorado as a young boy, and then again to Clifton, Colorado where he graduated from Palisade High School in 2003.

He was motivated to join the Marines by the events of September 11, 2001. Phelps was killed in action on April 9, 2004 (Good Friday) at the age of 19, outside Ramadi, Iraq. Phelps's unit was conducting convoy escort when they came under heavy small arms afire, including rocket-propelled grenades. Despite being wounded, he refused to be evacuated, and instead manned his M240 machine gun, also reported to have been a M2 .50 caliber machine gun to cover the evacuation of the rest of his convoy. Upon withdrawal, he sustained his fatal wound to the head.

Sergeant Major Joseph Ellis, 40, of Ashland, Ohio, was the sergeant major of Battalion Landing Team, 2nd Battalion, 4th Marine Regiment, 15th Marine Expeditionary Unit, a part of Camp Pendleton's I Marine Expeditionary Force when he was killed February 7, 2007, in Iraq's Anbar province, west of Baghdad.

Ellis joined the Marines in 1984 and moved up the enlisted ranks, mostly in reconnaissance units. He served in Saudi Arabia during Operation Desert Storm, and later served in Hawaii, North Carolina and on Camp Pendleton. He served as a radio operator and supervisor in Japan, and a communications instructor for an infantry school on Camp Pendleton. After spending more than a year in the Middle East during the first Gulf War, he returned to Camp Pendleton as a company communications chief. He served a recruiting duty stint in Cleveland, just north of his hometown of Ashland, for three years, and then served a tour in Hawaii as a radio chief and a battalion communications chief.

As he continued to move through the ranks, he served as an infantry school instructor until the start of the Iraq war in 2003, when he returned to Iraq with the 2nd Battalion, 4th Marines. He was named the battalion's sergeant major in December of 2004. Ellis' awards include the Meritorious Service Medal, the Navy and Marine Corps Commendation Medal with combat distinction and one gold star, the Navy and Marine Corps Achievement Medal with one gold star and the Combat Action Ribbon with one gold star.

Major Megan Malia McClung graduated from the United States Naval Academy and was commissioned a Second Lieutenant in the United States Marine Corps in May 1995. After The Basic School, she completed the Public Affairs Officer Qualification Course, Ft. Meade, Maryland. In 1996, Major McClung reported to Marine Corps Base Camp Pendleton where she served as the Public Affairs Officer and Media Officer; provided PA support to Special Operations Training Group, and served as Executive Officer, Support Company, Headquarters and Support Battalion.

In 2004, McClung took a civilian position in public relations for Kellogg, Brown, and Root in Baghdad, Iraq. While there, she handled 31 fatalities; public relations preparation for Congressional hearings; and escorted media throughout the theater. When her one-year contract was complete, Major McClung returned stateside and went on active duty with U.S. Marine Corps Forces, Atlantic, as the Deputy PAO.

In October 2005, McClung was mobilized to active duty with the 1st Marine Expeditionary Force and deployed to Al Anbar Province, Iraq, in February 2006.

She was the Public Affairs Plans Officer at Camp Fallujah when she volunteered for duty with the Army's 1st Brigade, 1st Armored Division, operating in Ramadi. She was killed when her Humvee struck an improvised explosive device after escorting a FOX News crew to the Governance Center, and a Newsweek reporter to a Coalition outpost in the city.

Major McClung held a Bachelor of Science degree in General Science from the U.S. Naval Academy and completed her Master's degree in Criminal Justice through Boston University. Her awards include The Bronze Star, Purple Heart, Navy and Marine Corps Commendation Medal, and National Defense Service Medal.

Major McClung was an avid marathon runner and triathlete. As a triathlete, she competed in seven Ironman distance triathlons. Her accomplishments include winning the First Military Female award in Kona in 2000 and placing second the next year. She organized the first Marine Corps Marathon (Forward) in Iraq to coincide with the 2006 Marine Corps Marathon and served as the Race Director. Despite running with an injury, she placed second among the female runners.

Major McClung was the daughter of Michael and Re McClung of Coupeville, Washington. She is buried in Section 60 at Arlington National Cemetery.

Major Douglas Zembiec graduated from the United States Naval Academy and was commissioned as a Second Lieutenant in the U.S. Marine Corps in 1995. After finishing The Basic School, and the Infantry Officer's Course, he was assigned to 1st Battalion, 6th Marines as a rifle platoon commander in Bravo Company, which was effective starting April 1996. After successfully passing the Force Reconnaissance indoctrination in June 1997, he was transferred to 2nd Force Reconnaissance Company, at Camp Lejeune, North Carolina.

As part of his training for Force Reconnaissance, he completed Army Airborne School as well as the Marine Combatant Diver Course. He served for two and a half years as a platoon commander, eight months as an interim company commander, and one month as an operations officer. Zembiec's Force Reconnaissance platoon was among the first special operations forces to enter Kosovo during Operation Joint Guardian in June 1999.

In September 2000, he was transferred to the Amphibious Reconnaissance School (ARS) located in Ft. Story, Virginia and served as the Assistant Officer-In-Charge (AOIC) for two years. In 2001, Zembiec competed in the Armed Forces Eco-Challenge as team captain of Team Force Recon Rolls Royce.

From ARS, Zembiec was selected to attend the Marine Corps' Expeditionary Warfare School in Quantico, Virginia, graduating in May 2003. Following the Expeditionary Warfare School he took command of Company E, 2nd Battalion, 1st Marine Regiment, 1st Marine Division in July 2003.

He was named the "Lion of Fallujah" as a result of his heroic actions leading Echo Company 2/1 during Operation Vigilant Resolve in 2004. As a rifle company commander, he led 168 Marines and Sailors in the first conventional ground assault into Fallujah, Iraq. He was awarded a Silver Star, Bronze Star with Combat Distinguishing Device and two Purple Hearts due to wounds incurred in action.

He turned over command of Echo Company in November 2004 and served as an assistant operations officer at the Marine Corps' First Special Operations Training Group (1st SOTG) where he ran the urban patrolling/ Military Operations in Urban Terrain (MOUT) and tank-infantry training packages for the 13th Marine Expeditionary Unit in preparation for an upcoming deployment to Iraq. Zembiec transferred from 1st SOTG to the Regional Support Element, Headquarters, Marine Corps on June 10, 2005. His promotion to Major was effective on July 1, 2005.

Zembiec was serving in the CIA's Special Activities Division Ground Branch in Iraq when he was killed by small arms fire while leading a raid in Baghdad on May 11, 2007. Zembiec was leading a unit of Iraqi forces he had helped train. Zembiec is buried in Section 60 at Arlington National Cemetery.

Sergeant Major Robert Cottle, assigned to the 4th Light Armored Reconnaissance Battalion, 4th Marine Division, Marine Forces Reserve, based out of Camp Pendleton, died March 24, 2010 while supporting combat operations in Helmand Province, Afghanistan.

While deployed in support of Operation Enduring Freedom, his unit was attached to Marine Expeditionary Brigade-Afghanistan. Cottle, 45, was on military leave from the Los Angeles Police Department where he served as an elite SWAT officer, when his vehicle was struck by an Improvised Explosive Device. The blast killed Cottle and another Marine. Cottle is buried in Section 60 at Arlington National Cemetery.

Christopher Antonik was a native of Crystal Lake, Illinois, and a 2001 graduate of Prairie Ridge High School. He enlisted in the Marine Corps in May 2001. He began his career as a Reconnaissance Marine, first with 3rd Reconnaissance Battalion in Okinawa, Japan, and then with 1st Recon Company at Camp Pendleton, California. Antonik was a parachutist and combat diver, and joined the Marine Corps' Special Operations Command in September 2009.

Antonik deployed in support of both Operations Iraqi Freedom and Enduring Freedom. He was conducting a cordon and search mission in Hyderabad, in Helmand Province, Afghanistan, on a foot patrol when he was killed by an Improvised Explosive Device. Antonik's personal decorations include Bronze Star with combat V, Purple Heart, Navy-Marine Corps Achievement Medal with combat V, two Combat Action Ribbons and three Good Conduct Medals.

Major Ricardo Crocker of Mission Viejo, California, was killed on May 26, 2005. He died from a rocket propelled grenade explosion while conducting combat operations in Hadithah, Iraq. Crocker was a reservist assigned to the Marine Force Reserve's 3rd Civil Affairs Group, based at Camp Pendleton, California. Crocker was a 10-year veteran of the Santa Monica Police Department.

Crocker's last assignment with the Santa Monica Police Department was with the Police Activities League, where he helped procure computers for a program to help prepare students for their college entrance exam. His memory has been memorialized by dedicating a portion of the Santa Monica 10 freeway in his honor.

SSGT DARIN HOOVER

NEVER FORGOTTEN
AUGUST 26, 2021 - KABUL, AFGHANISTAN

THEY SERVED WITH HONOR AND GAVE THEIR LIVES IN ORDER TO PROTECT AND SAVE OTHERS.

LCPL DAVID ESPINOZA

CPL HUNTER LOPEZ

LCPL RYLEE MCCOLLUM

LCPL DYLAN MEROLA

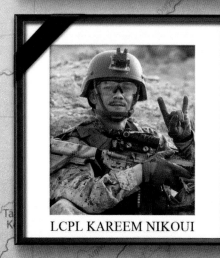

LCPL KAREEM NIKOUI

CPL DAEGAN PAGE

CPL HUMBERTO SANCHEZ

CPL JARED SCHMITZ

HM MAXTON SOVIAK

Graphic by Dan Zimmerman, Devil Dog Graphix

THE FINAL CHAPTER

The war in Afghanistan ended much as it began—with U.S. Marines defending a runway.

In 2001, Camp Pendleton Marines from 15th Marine Expeditionary Unit were some of the first conventional troops to land in Afghanistan after the attacks on 9/11. Nearly twenty years later, Marines found themselves far from home and in harm's way. Through the past two decades, just as they have since 1942, the surrounding communities have continued to support and care for our Marines, Sailors and their families.

The Camp Pendleton-based Marines and Sailor were part of 2nd Battalion, 1st Marine Regiment, part of the 1st Marine Division, the oldest and largest in the Corps. The battalion is known as The Professionals, and dates to the 1920s, when it participated in the occupation of the Dominican Republic. It has seen combat in almost every war since, including Korea, Vietnam, Iraq and Afghanistan.

Nine Marines and one Sailor based at Camp Pendleton were among the thirteen U.S. service members killed in a suicide bombing at Hamid Karzai International Airport in Kabul, Afghanistan, Aug. 26, 2021.

The nine Marines and one Sailor killed were:

Staff Sgt. Darin T. Hoover, 31, Salt Lake City, Utah

Cpl. Hunter Lopez, 22, Indio, California

Cpl. Daegan W. Page, 23, Omaha, Nebraska

Cpl. Humberto A. Sanchez, 22, Logansport, Indiana

Lance Cpl. Jared M. Schmitz, 20, St. Charles, Missouri

Lance Cpl. David L. Espinoza, 20, Rio Bravo, Texas

Lance Cpl. Rylee J. McCollum, 20, Jackson, Wyoming

Lance Cpl. Dylan R. Merola, 20, Rancho Cucamonga, California

Lance Cpl. Kareem M. Nikoui, 20, Norco, California

Navy Hospitalman Maxton W. Soviak, 22, Berlin Heights, Ohio

The front gate to Camp Pendleton turned into a temporary memorial to honor those killed by a suicide bomber at the Hamid Karzai International Airport in Kabul, Afghanistan. Flowers, U.S. flags, and other memorial items were placed there within hours of learning of the attack on Aug. 26, 2021.

Lance Cpl. Rylee
McCollum, 20, a Marine
from Bondurant, Wyo.

CHAPTER 7

CARING COMMUNITIES

SAN CLEMENTE

Park Semper Fi was dedicated on Nov. 12, 2005, at a ceremony organized by the Heritage of San Clemente Foundation and the City of San Clemente to commemorate the 230th birthday of the U.S. Marine Corps. The park features a life-size bronze statue of a Marine in the Dress Blue uniform that overlooks the San Clemente Pier. Community members from several organizations came together and designed a park that would offer a place to honor the special and unique relationship between the city and Marines from Camp Pendleton. Park Semper Fi is located in Parque Del Mar and can be accessed from N. Alameda Lane in San Clemente.

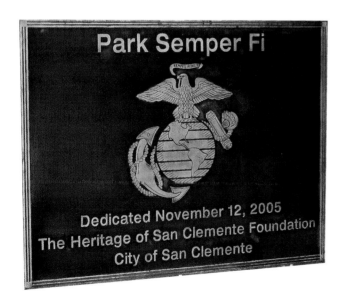

PARK SEMPER FI

BY G. WAYNE EGGLESTON, EXECUTIVE DIRECTOR, THE HERITAGE OF SAN CLEMENTE FOUNDATION AND FORMER CITY COUNCIL MEMBER & MAYOR

The United States Marine Corps has been a valuable neighbor of San Clemente since the early 1940s when the Marine base was established and dedicated by President Franklin D. Roosevelt. This community has seen Marines pass through our town during World War II, the Korean War, Vietnam War, and the Gulf War. They have been our neighbors, sons, daughters, husbands, wives and community leaders. As a community, we have honored them with barbecues and parades, and now we honor them as a permanent reminder of our respect and appreciation for them.

The Board of The Heritage of San Clemente Foundation, a non-profit organization 501(c)3, now honors them in a manner that is a permanent reminder that their heroism is an important part of San Clemente's heritage. Therefore, we launched a private fund raising drive to erect a Marine Corps Monument in San Clemente. The community was asked what type of statue would be appropriate and they have chosen the Dress Blue Uniform as the one that is most symbolic of The United States Marine Corps. It is a life-sized bronze statue placed in the newly created Park Semper Fi located in the Pier Bowl where residents and visitors alike can view it. The Monument was dedicated on Saturday, November 12, 2005 at noon in commemoration of the Marine Corps 230th Birthday.

The Monument will, for all time, attest to the Corp's honor, courage, and commitment in service to our nation. This is a once-in-a-lifetime opportunity for us to come together to honor the Marines, to confirm our heritage, to share with our community, and with each other, and to leave a lasting and glorious legacy for the future.

6 August 2019

Dear Mr. Eggleston,

As you host this year's *Park Semper Fi* Veterans Day celebration, I want to take this opportunity to thank you for your exceptional support of the Marines, Sailors, and families stationed at Marine Corps Base Camp Pendleton. We greatly appreciate everything you do to promote good relations between the San Clemente community and the military members and families in your area.

From scheduling and promoting pre-deployment picnics and post-deployment welcome home events, to advocating for the city to adopt Camp Pendleton units, you are consistently the driving force behind taking care of our warriors. Your vision and leadership played a crucial role in bringing the *Park Semper Fi* concept to life, complete with the distinctive Marine Monument as the centerpiece.

On behalf of all Marines, I extend deepest gratitude for your support and your tireless efforts to strengthen the relationship between our military and San Clemente. Thank you for being a great friend to our Corps and helping us with one of our most important missions – taking care of our Marines and their families.

Semper Fidelis,

David H. Berger
General, U.S. Marine Corps
Commandant of the Marine Corps

Mr. G. Wayne Eggleston
Executive Director, The Heritage of San Clemente Foundation
P.O. Box 456
San Clemente, CA 92674

TEMECULA

The Temecula Fallen Heroes Memorial, located at the Temecula Duck Pond alongside the Path of Honor, is the most recent addition to the city's ongoing efforts to recognize the importance of military service in the community.

The Fallen Heroes Memorial features multiple elements, including a life-size battlefield cross cast in bronze, and a life-size bald eagle forged in steel and mounted in the attack position on top of a 17-foot tall steel tower. Arranged in front of the tower on the ground are five bronze military service seals honoring the individual branches of the U.S. Armed Services.

A retaining wall partially surrounds the memorial, and U.S. and California flags fly behind the tower. The group selected a site at the Duck Pond to complement the existing *Letters Home* Memorial and Path of Honor, and Sculptor Austin Casson was invited to provide design concepts for the memorial to honor all Temecula residents who were killed in the line of duty. The Fallen Heroes Memorial was unveiled at a ribbon cutting on Nov. 8, 2018, and remains one of Temecula's most visible tributes to its military community and the sacrifice service members make. The memorial is located at 28250 Rancho California Road in Temecula, California.

FALLEN HEROES

This monument bears witness
to the City of Temecula's Fallen Heroes,
those courageous few who have died
in military service to our country.

The City dedicates this memorial as a record
of their sacrifice and of our gratitude,
that those who visit may help ensure
their legacies endure.

*"A hero is someone who has given his or her life
to something bigger than oneself."*
Joseph Campbell

In 1993, the city of Temecula became sister cities with Daisen-Nakayama, Japan, and with Leidschendam-Voorburg, Netherlands. Temecula's duck pond space honors the traditions and beauty of Japan with distinctly unique Japanese architecture, plants and sculptures that are representations of the country's artistic style. The inspiration for the memorial came in the wake of March 19, 2016, when Temecula resident and U.S. Marine Staff Sgt. Louis Cardin, a 27-year-old field artilleryman was tragically killed in action in Iraq while supporting Operation Inherent Resolve, the U.S. military's campaign against ISIS.

Cardin was praised for his valor in ensuring the safety of his fellow soldiers when he was killed.

Prompted by this loss, the Military Ad Hoc Subcommittee requested that staff coordinate an effort with community partners including the Veterans of Foreign Wars Post 4089, the Temecula Valley Woman's Club, Commissioner Bob Hagel, and Riverside County Supervisor Chuck Washington to discuss the possibility of creating a memorial to honor Staff Sgt. Louis Cardin. (Courtesy photo)

Marines with 2nd Battalion, 10th Marines, held a memorial ceremony for Staff Sgt. Louis F. Cardin at the Protestant Chapel aboard Marine Corps Base Camp Lejeune, North Carolina, July 14, 2016. Cardin was supporting Operation Inherent Resolve in Iraq when he was killed March 19 while serving as a member of Task Force Spartan. Task Force Spartan was composed of Marines from the 26th Marine Expeditionary Unit and was responsible for providing indirect fire support to Iraqi security forces near the town of Mosul. (U.S. Marine Corps photo by Staff Sgt. Bobby J. Yarbrough)

THIS MEMORIAL IS FOR THE MEN AND WOMEN
WHO HAD THE COURAGE TO STAND UP FOR THEIR BELIEFS
ANSWERING THE CALL OF THEIR NATION
AND RISKING THEIR LIVES TO PROTECT FREEDOM

THE PEOPLE OF TEMECULA
HONOR THEIR DEEDS

"LETTERS HOME" VETERANS MEMORIAL

The steps leading to the memorial and the wheelchair access ramp extending from the memorial are each dedicated as a "Path of Honor." The paths are made of permanent granite pavers, each engraved with the names of men or women who have served our nation in our Armed Forces during peace or war at any time in our history from the Revolutionary War through the current conflicts in Iraq and Afghanistan.

Located at the Temecula Duck Pond, the Letters Home Veterans Memorial, designed by Artist Christopher Pardell, is dedicated in honor of our veterans.

The "Path of Honor" was founded in 2004 by David Micheal, Photographer's Mate 1st Class, U.S. Navy, a decorated World War II veteran of the Iwo Jima campaign.

In commemoration of
Murrieta's proud Soldiers,
Sailors, Marines, and
Airmen who have made
the supreme sacrifice
in the defense of our
Nation. They will forever
be remembered and
honored by their
families, friends, and
this community over
which they continue
to stand faithful watch.

MURRIETA

Murrieta Town Square Park is home to a unique military memorial that reflects the strong patriotism and respect for service members and veterans that is prevalent throughout the community. A tall, granite obelisk stands proudly above a series of walls depicting dramatic and emotional imagery of our men and women who have served and sacrificed in our nation's defense. These memorials are located at 1 Town Square in Murrieta, California.

Veterans Memorial in Murrieta, California

CAMP PENDLETON

5th Marines Memorial Park and Garden
Camp San Mateo - 62 Area

It's a revered site and home to monuments and memorials honoring fallen Marines and Sailors from 5th Marines. It was designed in partnership with Dana Point 5th Marine Regiment Support Group as a place for fellow Marines and Sailors, their families and others who wish to pay their respects to those who've made the ultimate sacrifice.

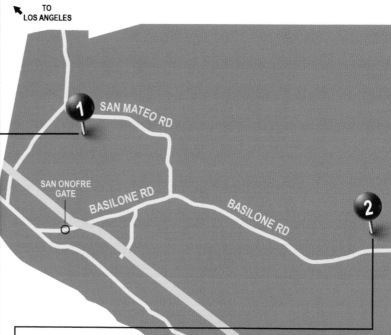

TO
LOS ANGELES

SAN MATEO RD

SAN ONOFRE
GATE

BASILONE RD

BASILONE RD

LAS PULGAS RD

PACIFIC
OCEAN

CAMP
DEL MAR
BEACH

1st Marines Memorial Park and Garden
Camp Horno - 53 Area

The 1st Marines Memorial Park was established in 2013 and was spearheaded by the Rotary Club of Camp Pendleton. The one-acre garden, with desert landscaping and mountain views, provides a quiet place to remember heroes of the regiment. The Memorial Park is a gathering place where many Regimental memories are made including celebrations and promotions.

Camp Pendleton Veterans Memorial Garden
Pacific Views Event Center

The Camp Pendleton Veterans Memorial Garden was dedicated on Aug. 21, 2003. The garden is located across from the Pacific Views Events Center and overlooks the ocean, serving as a quiet place for reflection. The garden honors historical actions or events of significance on behalf of active military units and veterans' organizations. The gardens contain many plants that are native to the region and are maintained by Marines, Navy and civilian volunteers.

Graphic by Dan Zimmerman, Devil Dog Graphix

MEMORIALS MAP

4

No Man Left Behind Statue
Wounded Warrior West Complex

The statue is located at the entrance to the Wounded Warrior Complex and was unveiled in 2014. The sculpture is from a photo taken by journalist Lucian Read depicting 1st Sgt. Brad Kasal, center, from a 2004 battle in Fallujah, Iraq. A similar sculpture is also placed at Camp Lejeune in North Carolina. The bronze statue was created by a gold star father, John Phelps, from Wyoming, who also served as a Marine in Vietnam.

5

I Marine Expeditionary Force Memorial Wall
Mainside at 11 Area Parade Field

The I Marine Expeditionary Force Memorial Wall was unveiled and dedicated by Lt. Gen. Thomas Waldhauser on February 1, 2012. More than 1,200 names of Marines who died in Iraq and Afghanistan since 9/11 are engraved on the curving stone wall located across the street from the 1st Marine Division headquarters building in Mainside at Camp Pendleton.

6

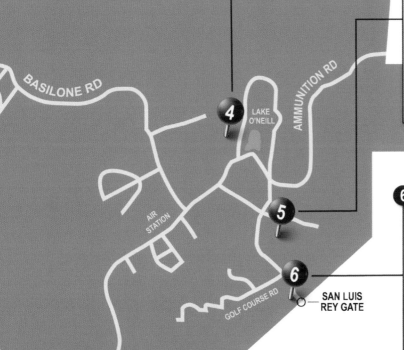

Military Working Dog Memorial
San Luis Rey Gate

The base's canine kennel complex, known as Camp Cann, is named after Sgt. Adam Cann, a 23-year-old from Destin, Florida, who was killed in Ramadi, Iraq, in 2006. Cann was based at Camp Pendleton and the first dog handler killed in action since Vietnam. The memorial is made from a "Texas Barrier" wall that was originally painted at Camp Fallujah, Iraq, and brought back to the U.S.

BASILONE RD

AMMUNITION RD

4 LAKE O'NEILL

AIR STATION

5

6 SAN LUIS REY GATE

GOLF COURSE RD

STUART MESA RD

OCEANSIDE

3

21 AREA MARINA

MAIN GATE

TO SAN DIEGO

HEROES LIVE HERE

The Camp Pendleton Historical Society, a non-profit organization, was instrumental in restoring the 19th-century wagon to it's current condition. Its stands in the heart of Camp Pendleton at the entrance to the nearly 200-year-old Rancho Santa Margarita Ranch House and can be seen by anyone driving along Vandergrift Blvd. The symbolic wagon goes back to Camp Pendleton's pre-base days when the area was one of the largest cattle ranches in California.

ACKNOWLEDGMENTS

I'd like to thank my family for their continued support and encouragement through the years and for always "holding down the fort" so I could deploy and serve our country in a foreign land.

To my husband, **Dieter,** thank you for believing I could actually write a book and for encouraging me when I wanted to quit. Thanks for brainstorming ideas with me to make this a meaningful project and for keeping me on track for the past six months.

My deepest gratitude goes to those who shared their personal reflections and images to help preserve the history and memory our fallen Marines and Sailors with ties to Camp Pendleton:

Lt. Gen. Lawrence Nicholson

Col. Greg Martin

Col. Bryan Salas

Lt. Col. Alex Durr

Sgt. Maj. Justin LeHew

Master Sgt. Robert Blanton

Michael Dowling

Terry Rifkin

Frank Sellin

G. Wayne Eggleston

Your contributions and support for this project means the world to me and my hope is that this book will bring comfort and reassurance to fellow Marines, friends and family members of those lost in Iraq and Afghanistan. Your strong ties to the Camp Pendleton community and surrounding area is a testament to your lifelong commitment to service and desire for making an impact wherever you can.

To **Bo Hellman** of the Camp Pendleton Historical Society, thank you for helping me share the important history of Camp Pendleton through the beautiful collection of images that are preserved by the Camp Pendleton History & Museum Division.

To **Trish Beaulieu** and **Nancy Ratkiewich,** at NJR Productions, thank you for your patience and expertise in coaching me through the editing, design, and production of this book. I'm so grateful for your expertise in getting me across the finish line.

To **Dan Zimmerman**, a fellow Marine veteran and graphic designer for the book, thank you for seeing the vision for the book before I could even write it. Your passion for this project shines through with your amazing graphics and makes this book a true 'work of art.'

To **Marcy Browe,** branding expert and photographer, thank you for starting me on this journey and cheering me on along the way! Your creative vision and trust in me set the stage to share this project with our community and a wider audience. Thank you for your beautiful images and connecting me with your supportive network.

A special thanks to **Susie Schaefer,** owner of Finish The Book Publishing, who shared her expertise and guided me through this long and detailed process. Thank you for taking on this project and coaching me along this new journey, which has allowed me to spread my wings in ways I never thought possible. I'm grateful for your passion in guiding independent authors from concept to completion, while helping them retain greater creative control.

The following pages are resources and non-profit organizations that I know are dedicated to helping our servicemembers, their families and our veteran community. I'm proud to showcase them here as trusted resources for those who may need it. I'm proud to donate a portion of the book proceeds to *The Semper Fi & America's Fund,* one of the original organizations that began assisting Marines and their family members based at Camp Pendleton at the beginning of Operation Iraqi Freedom in 2003.

ABOUT THE AUTHOR

Amy Forsythe is an award-winning multimedia journalist and military combat veteran with nearly 30 years of experience in storytelling, communications, and multimedia content creation.

She served nearly 18 years in the U.S. Marine Corps, on active duty, and in the reserves, as a Combat Correspondent (MOS: 4341/4313) with multiple deployments, including two deployments to Iraq and three to Afghanistan. In 2010, she transferred from the Marine Corps Reserve to the U.S. Navy Reserve.

Her overseas deployments also include positions with Joint Special Operations Command, U.S. Africa Command, and the DoD's Media Bureau Chief on Guam for nearly five years.

Amy was stationed on Camp Pendleton for many years beginning in 1995 and served as a reporter for *The Scout Newspaper* and an anchor and producer for the award-winning *Pendleton Journal* television program. During her assignment at I Marine Expeditionary Force, she served in various public affairs leadership roles that included coordinating community relations events, tours of the base, and media engagement activities.

Through the years, her photos, video, and articles have been widely published on *Fox News Channel, CNN, MSNBC, ABC News, Newsweek* magazine, *Soldier of Fortune* magazine, *Leatherneck* magazine, and many other news outlets.

A native of Santa Rosa, California, Amy joined the U.S. Marines in 1993 and spent eight years on active duty before transitioning to a successful career in the media industry. Amy created, produced, and anchored a lifestyle television program called "North County's Endless Summer" for *KOCT* and later worked as a reporter for *NBC 7* San Diego. She was also hand-selected to be an anchor and correspondent for *The Pentagon Channel* from 2003 to 2010.

Amy currently serves as a Public Affairs Officer in the U.S. Navy Reserve, advising and leading strategic communications activities at various commands. Amy holds a Bachelor of Arts degree in Communications from California State University at San Marcos and a Master's of Science in Global Leadership from the University of San Diego. She has also a proud graduate of several courses at The Defense Information School at Fort Meade, Maryland.

Residing in north San Diego County with her husband and their rescue dog, Schatzie, Amy enjoys hiking local trails and golfing many nearby courses. Amy still has strong ties to Camp Pendleton and the surrounding communities.

ORDER

A SIGNED HARDCOVER BOOK

HEROES LIVE HERE

A TRIBUTE TO CAMP PENDLETON MARINES SINCE 9/11

Order *Heroes Live Here* or make a donation to purchase books for Gold Star families, local schools and military units.

SEMPER FI & AMERICA'S®
F U N D

A portion of the proceeds from the sale of this book will be donated to the Semper Fi & America's Fund.

www.heroeslivehere.com

RESOURCES

Semper Fi & America's Fund

Dana Point 5th Marine
Regiment Support Group

Camp Pendleton Historical Society

History Flight

Soul Survivor Outdoor

Women Marine Association/
Edith Macias Vann Southern
California Chapter CA-7

United American Patriots

Warfighter Made

Navy and Marine Corps
P.R.O.U.D. Foundation

Warrior Foundation
Freedom Station

Operation Game On

The Station Foundation

The Warrior Connection

The Honor Foundation

Screaming Eagle Aviation Association

Night Stalker Foundation

Force Blue

Elite Meet

Hunter Seven Foundation

Marine Reconnaissance Foundation

Operation Sacred Promise

Military Women's Memorial

Special Operations
Warrior Foundation

The Rosie Network

United States Marine Corps Combat
Correspondents Association

Mt. Soledad National
Veterans Memorial

Foundation for Women Warriors

1st Marine Division Association

Devil Dog Graphix

Sellin Photography

Connect with
Amy Forsythe, Author

*The following pages feature 30 organizations that were carefully selected
based on a strong personal connection to the author and are uniquely
dedicated to serving our military and veteran communities.*

PROUD SUPPORTER

SEMPER FI & AMERICA'S
FUND

For Our Combat Wounded, Ill, and Injured

The Semper Fi & America's Fund is dedicated to providing immediate financial assistance and lifetime support to combat wounded, critically ill and catastrophically injured members of all branches of the U.S. Armed Forces and their families. We deliver the resources they need during recovery and transition back to their communities, working to ensure no one is left behind.

www.TheFund.org
(760) 725-3680

*A portion of the book proceeds will be donated to Semper Fi & America's Fund

Join us in Preserving a Historic San Diego County Treasure...

Camp Pendleton

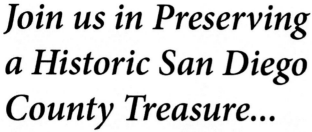

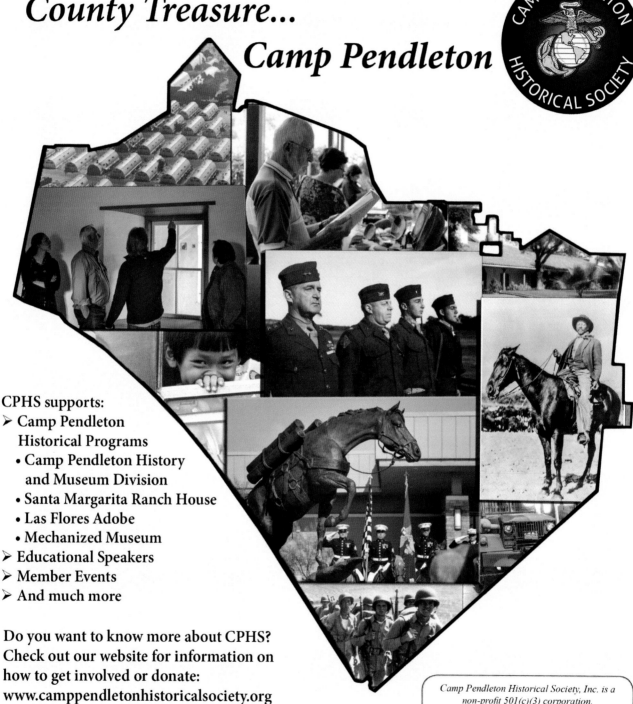

CPHS supports:
- ➢ Camp Pendleton
  Historical Programs
  - • Camp Pendleton History
    and Museum Division
  - • Santa Margarita Ranch House
  - • Las Flores Adobe
  - • Mechanized Museum
- ➢ Educational Speakers
- ➢ Member Events
- ➢ And much more

Do you want to know more about CPHS?
Check out our website for information on
how to get involved or donate:
www.camppendletonhistoricalsociety.org

Follow us and like us on Facebook
www.facebook.com/camppendletonhistoricalsociety/

*Camp Pendleton Historical Society, Inc. is a
non-profit 501(c)(3) corporation.*

*Camp Pendleton Historical Society is a non-
Federal entity. It is not a part of the Department
of Defense or any of its components and
it has no governmental status.*

Women Marines Association
VISION STATEMENT

The Women Marines Association (WMA) will be the veterans' organization of choice for female Marines (past, present, and future) looking for camaraderie, mentoring, and support. The Women Marines Association is proud to be the only charitable association for and about women Marines. WMA is a non-profit 501(c)3 charitable organization.

The Women Marines Association, Edith Macias Vann - SoCal Chapter CA-7 is located in Oceanside, CA. Our meetings are the 2nd Saturday of each month (except July and August) held at Veterans Association of North County (VANC) located at 1617 Mission Ave, Oceanside, CA, 92058.

To become a member of this chapter, you must be a member of the National Women Marines Association (www.womenmarines.org).

WMA CA-7 is involved in serving our local community by:
- Providing 3 local high school seniors with scholarships
- Volunteering our time for the food drive at Veterans Association of North County (VANC)
- Donating money to other charities that support local military community
- Presenting the history of Women Marines aboard Camp Pendleton to various units
- Participating in parades and ceremonies

For more information, visit our website and social media:
www.womenmarines.net
Facebook: wmasocalca7
Instagram: ca7womenmarines

UAP Generates Public Awareness, Funds Legal Representation, and Provides Reintegration Support For Our Nation's Warriors To Preserve Our Rights, Defend Our Defenders, and Enhance Our Communities.

CONTACT INFO:
WWW.UAP.ORG
EMAIL: INFO@UAP.ORG
PHONE: 571-366-1835

David "BULL" Gurfein, Lt. Col., USMCR (Ret.)
Vice-Chairman of the Board and CEO

WARFIGHTER MADE
provides recreational therapy to ill, injured, and combat wounded veterans and service members.

WARFIGHTER MADE

WWW.WARFIGHTERMADE.ORG

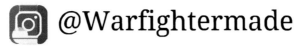 @Warfightermade

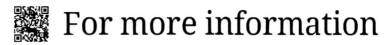 www.facebook.com/warfightermade

For more information

 Robert Blanton is a Force Recon Marine, Scout Sniper and Silver Star recipient, who served 21 years in the Marine Corps. He founded Warfighter Made in 2013 as a way to continue his service to our veteran community.

Navy Marine Corps P.R.O.U.D. Foundation

"Please Remember Our Unwavering Devotion"

The Navy Marine Corps P.R.O.U.D. Foundation is a nonprofit organization providing financial and in-kind support to San Diego County's Navy Marine Corps Relief Society programs & local active duty Sailors, Marines, Veterans, Retirees and their families in need.

To learn more, visit

navymarinecorpsproudfoundation.org

or contact us at info@nmcpf.org

WARRIOR FOUNDATION
FREEDOM STATION®

Proudly Serving Our Local San Diego Warriors

Founded in 2004, Warrior Foundation Freedom Station is a leading force in assisting, honoring and supporting the military men and women who have bravely served and sacrificed for our country. We are committed to supporting both active duty and medically retired warriors with quality-of-life items, support services and transitional housing that assist them and their families during recovery. Warrior Foundation Freedom Station is a nonprofit 501(c)3 organization that proudly holds a four-star rating from Charity Navigator, that nation's largest evaluator of charities.

Transitional Housing Residences at Freedom Station I and II

Education & Career Guidance

Vocational Projects

Adaptive Sports and Wheelchair Basketball

Outdoor Therapy Programs

Post-Traumatic Stress Treatment

Quality of Life Items and much more…

We are proud to provide San Diego's injured military men and women with hope, a home and a chance to start the next chapter of their lives with the honor and dignity befitting the world's finest fighting forces.

WWW.WARRIORFOUNDATION.ORG
(619) 578-2615

OPERATION GAME ON

"Building confidence once swing at a time"

Tony Perez, President/Founder
Vietnam Veteran, U.S. Air Force

MORE INFO

operationgameon.org

The mission of OGO is to provide golf as a form of rehabilitation for returning combat injured men and women Veterans, suffering from severe physical and mental disabilities sustained in combat while deployed in Iraq and Afghanistan.

The Station™ provides a remote Montana sanctuary where
SOF Families and Gold Star Children recharge, reconnect, and refocus
on a virtuous life of meaning and purpose.

THE STATION FOUNDATION® **406.763.5505**   info@thestationfoundation.org

 www.facebook.com/TheStationFoundation   twitter.com/THESTATIONfndn

1627 West Main St. Suite #258   Bozeman, MT 59715

THE STATION®
FOUNDATION
A CRUCIAL STOP ON THE JOURNEY HOME

The Warrior Connection

The Warrior Connection (TWC) provides residential retreats and services to Veterans and their families to heal the invisible injuries incurred while in uniform. Our retreats are run by Veterans, teamed with licensed clinicians and Veteran mentors. Since TWC's inception in 2010, **not a single graduate** has been lost to suicide.

All TWC programs and services are open to Veterans of all eras. Thanks to our donors, sponsors, and volunteers, retreats are offered at no cost with fully covered travel expenses to veterans and military spouses from all 50 states.

If you, or a Veteran or military spouse you know is struggling, please reach out or share our resources.

WarriorConnection.org

After a career in Special Operations, what's next?

We exist so this question does not go unanswered without 100% purpose and clarity.

The Honor Foundation (THF) is a career transition program for U.S. Special Operations Forces that effectively translates their elite military service to the private sector and helps create the next generation of corporate and community leaders. We're standing by to "serve you with honor for life, so your next mission is clear and continues to impact the world."

THE HONOR FOUNDATION
honor.org

SCREAMING EAGLE AVIATION ASSOCIATION

Mission:

The Screaming Eagle Aviation Association supports Screaming Eagle Aviation Soldiers, family members and memorializes those that made the ultimate sacrifice. We execute through not for profit fund raising.

Purpose:

The objective of the Screaming Eagle Aviation Association is to provide for the health, comfort, welfare, and morale of Soldiers assigned or attached to 101st Combat Aviation Brigade.

★ Support memorial services for deceased Soldiers to include support for their family members

★ Support wounded, injured and ill Soldiers to include their family members

★ Provide necessary comfort and aid to 101st CAB Soldiers and family members. Any funds generated or deposited with this organization may be used to pay for health, comfort, welfare, and morale items for Soldiers and their families.

Supporting
Screaming Eagle Aviation Soldiers
and Their Families

 Message us on Facebook for more information @101seaa.

No funds will be given directly to Soldiers or their families for their own use. All items purchased by the fund must be approved by the governing body, and should be distributed equally and without regard to rank or position, to the extent feasible and reasonable, among deployed Soldiers and their families, regardless of rank or position.

NIGHT STALKER FOUNDATION

SOLDIERS & FAMILIES
FAMILIES OF THE FALLEN
COLLEGE SCHOLARSHIPS
PRESERVE THE LEGACY

ALWAYS REMEMBER

"Serving Those Who Serve"

The Night Stalker Foundation
is a best-in-class charitable non-profit group
fully supporting the needs of current
and former Soldiers and Families of the 160th Special Operations Aviation Regiment.

nightstalkerfoundation.com

GIVING WARRIORS A CAUSE. GIVING A CAUSE ITS WARRIORS.

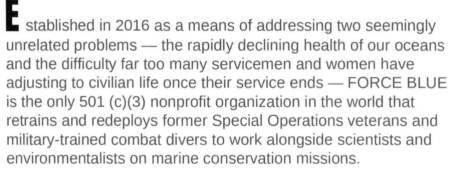

Established in 2016 as a means of addressing two seemingly unrelated problems — the rapidly declining health of our oceans and the difficulty far too many servicemen and women have adjusting to civilian life once their service ends — FORCE BLUE is the only 501 (c)(3) nonprofit organization in the world that retrains and redeploys former Special Operations veterans and military-trained combat divers to work alongside scientists and environmentalists on marine conservation missions.

Harkening back to the days of Jacques Cousteau and the French frogmen he trained, FORCE BLUE has assembled a modern-day cadre of elite military veterans with the aptitude and ability to achieve great things on the conservation front — and the visibility to let the world know about it. Through its composition and commitment, FORCE BLUE is building a model of caring, cooperation and positive change with the power to restore lives and the planet.

If you believe in our mission and would like to play a part in its success, please visit **www.forceblueteam.org** or follow us **@forceblueteam**

ONE TEAM. ONE FIGHT.

ELITE MEET

Elite Meet is a 501(c)(3) organization that supports members of the various

SPECIAL OPERATIONS COMMUNITIES

as they transition from military service by connecting them with

LEADERS IN THE BUSINESS SECTOR.

A network-centric organization, Elite Meet promotes the extraordinary value and leadership experience of elite transitioning Veterans to premier organizations through a series of conferences, events and a digital community.

WWW.ELITEMEET.US | INFO@ELITEMEET.US | TAX I.D. # 82-3048668

HUNTERSEVEN FOUNDATION

Our mission is to research military exposures and their impact on the health of the veteran population, with the intention of sharing the data with the veteran and healthcare communities through education to

INCREASE AWARENESS OF EXPOSURES AND THE IMPACT ON VETERAN HEALTH.

HunterSeven Foundation, a veteran-founded, federally-recognized 501(c)(3) nonprofit organization that specializes in medical research and education specifically on the post-9/11 veteran cohort. The HunterSeven Foundation has quickly become the leaders in identifying potential toxic exposures and subsequent illnesses in military veterans and in turn is able to educate both the veteran population and the healthcare providers who care for them on critical health information relating to their exposures utilizing evidence-based practice.

HUNTERSEVEN.ORG | INFO@HUNTERSEVEN.ORG | EIN #83-1983697

The Marine Reconnaissance Foundation is committed to providing reoccurring annual programs, emergent/emergency support to our teammates past & present, as well as perpetuating the rich history, lineage and traditions of the Reconnaissance community.

reconfoundation.org   MRF is a registered 501(c)(3)
Tax ID# 46-3009425

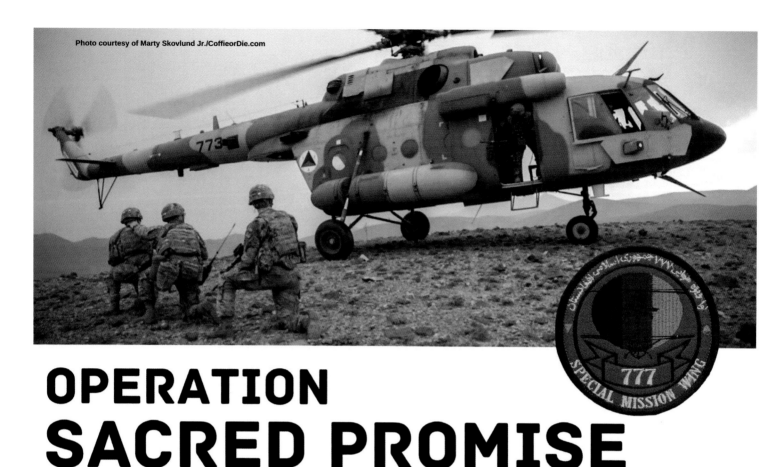

OPERATION SACRED PROMISE

The Operation Sacred Promise (OSP) mission is to honor the service and sacrifice of Afghan Air Force and Army Special Mission Wing warriors and their families by supporting their transition from Afghanistan and helping them build new, productive lives in the U.S. OSP provides consular assistance and resettlement support, including housing and basic life needs, job placement, language training, and cultural acclimation, in addition to ongoing advocacy and awareness efforts.

When you partner with OSP, you're helping Afghanistan Air Force members, Special Mission Wing members, and their families evacuate unsafe conditions and integrate into the U.S.

opsacredpromise.org

Dave Hicks, Founder of OSP
Served as an Air Force fighter pilot and retired after 30 years as a Brigadier General on the Air Force HQ Staff in the Pentagon.

Military Women's Memorial

The Military Women's Memorial is located at the entrance to Arlington National Cemetery, honors and tells the stories of women, past and present, who serve our nation.

Without **HER**story our nation's history is incomplete

The Military Women's Memorial is the only historical repository documenting all military women's service, we educate and inspire through innovative and interactive exhibitions, our world-class collections, and engaging programs and events for all generations. We honor the commitment, contributions and experiences of every woman who serves in, or with, the Armed Forces.

www.womensmemorial.org

Take your rightful place in history.
Scan the QR Code with your cell phone to
Register **HER**story

REGISTER

HER STORY *today!*

Join the thousands of women who have registered their **HER**story with the Military Women's Memorial

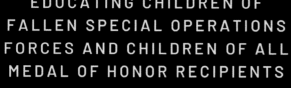

EDUCATING CHILDREN OF FALLEN SPECIAL OPERATIONS FORCES AND CHILDREN OF ALL MEDAL OF HONOR RECIPIENTS

S O W F

SPECIAL OPERATIONS WARRIOR FOUNDATION

Special Operations Warrior Foundation, a 41-year-old organization, provides fully funded educations to the surviving children of Special Operations Forces (Army, Navy, Air Force and Marine Corps) lost in the line of duty as well as children of all Medal of Honor recipients.

SOWF also provides immediate financial assistance to severely wounded, ill, and injured Special Operations Personnel.

For education, funds include:

- Fully funded college tuition, room/board, and miscellaneous expenses;
- Educational programs specifically designed for students with disabilities;
- Preschool programs for children ages 2-5;
- Unlimited private tutoring for students of all ages;
- Access to online college planning tools;
- Exclusive college planning conference; and
- College-to-Career transition programs.

FOR MORE INFO, VISIT: SPECIALOPS.ORG OR CALL (813) 805-9400

1188	**814**	**431**	**1166**	**1527**
WARRIOR FATALITIES	CHILDREN CURRENTLY ELIGIBLE	COLLEGE GRADUATES	SEVERELY WOUNDED, ILL & INJURED	SURVIVING CHILDREN

Totals as of October, 2021

Proud Supporter

The Rosie Network's mission is to build stronger military families by developing entrepreneurial programs and support services that empower active-duty, veterans and military spouses to realize the American Dream of small business ownership, increasing financial stability and self-sufficiency of those who have served our country.

SERVICE CEO

An entrepreneurship program for veterans, military spouses and active duty service members

www.TheRosieNetwork.org

501(C)3 PUBLICLY SUPPORTED NONPROFIT

Federal Tax ID Number: 46-1522625

Serving U.S. Marine Corps communicators, journalists, photographers, artists and broadcasters since 1947

Light typing required...

The United States Marines Corps Combat Correspondents Association (USMCCCA) and Foundation serves its members, and assists the U. S. Marine Corps and related agencies, to promote the professional development of its Communication Operations and Strategy members. In addition, we annually recognize the achievements of Marines and civilians who help to tell the Marine Corps story.

We are a not for profit organization.

www.usmccca.org | hq@usmccca.org | twitter: @usmccca
instagram.com/usmccca_org | linkedin.com/in/usmccca
facebook: facebook.com/usmccca

FOUNDATION FOR WOMEN WARRIORS

HONOR HER SERVICE | EMPOWER HER FUTURE

Our mission is to serve women veterans and their children so that their next mission is clear and continues to impact the world. Our programs address the growing needs of the increasing population of military women transitioning to civilian life.

"Foundation for Women Warriors provided me childcare assistance, mentorship, and so much more. If it were not for this amazing foundation, I would not be a college graduate today. I recently accepted a new job and am now enrolled in a master's program."

— Rebecca O., USMC Veteran

WOULD YOU LIKE TO SUPPORT WOMEN VETERANS?

Visit our website to learn more:
FOUNDATIONFORWOMENWARRIORS.ORG

Foundation for Women Warriors is a 501(c)3 non-profit organization Tax ID no. 20-5523954, contributions are fully tax-deductible.

1ST MARINE DIVISION ASSOCIATION

The 1st Marine Division Association (FMDA) is a non-profit organization dedicated to supporting active duty and retired Marines and Sailors of the 1st Marine Division and their families.

Contact us at: june.oldbreed@fmda.us
Phone: (760)763-3268
www.1stMarineDivisionAssociation.org
P.O Box 9000, PMB#902
Oceanside, California   92051-9000

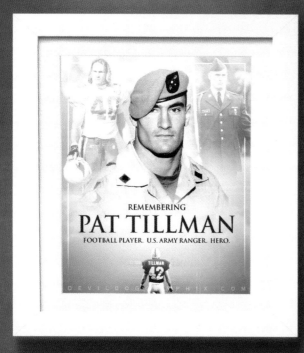

Sellin Photography

Frank Sellin is a Marine Corps infantry sergeant-turned amateur photographer. A portion of the profits from the sale of imagery will be donated to veterans organizations that he works with. If you're a veteran, active duty military, first responder or a Gold Star family member and would like one of the prints, please contact him to discuss additional discounts.

Many of the pictures that Frank takes are of various military aircraft and memorials. He also has an extensive collection of scenic, car and animal pictures. If you are looking for a custom photograph, contact him directly at fssellin@sellinphotography.com.

Frank's imagery can be found at:

 www.facebook.com/sellinphotography

 @sellinphotograph

px frank-sellin.pixels.com

Connect with me...

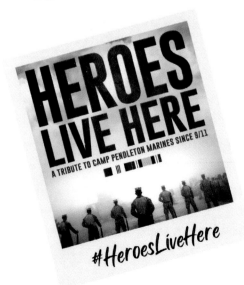

#HeroesLiveHere

#HeroesLiveHere

www.heroeslivehere.com